Windows 7: Basic

Student Manual

Windows 7: Basic

President, Axzo Press:	Jon Winder
Vice President, Product Development:	Charles G. Blum
Vice President, Operations:	Josh Pincus
Director of Publishing Systems Development:	Dan Quackenbush
Writer:	Don Tremblay
Copyeditor:	Catherine Oliver
Keytester:	Cliff Coryea

Student Manual
ISBN 10: 1-4260-1809-6
ISBN 13: 978-1-4260-1809-1

Student Manual with data CD
ISBN-10: 1-4260-1811-8
ISBN-13: 978-1-4260-1811-4

Printed in the United States of America

2 3 4 5 6 7 8 9 10 GL 13 12 11 10

Contents

Introduction

After reading this introduction, you will know how to:

A Use ILT Series manuals in general.

B Use prerequisites, a target student description, course objectives, and a skills inventory to properly set your expectations for the course.

C Re-key this course after class.

Topic A: About the manual

ILT Series philosophy

Our manuals facilitate your learning by providing structured interaction with the software itself. While we provide text to explain difficult concepts, the hands-on activities are the focus of our courses. By paying close attention as your instructor leads you through these activities, you will learn the skills and concepts effectively.

We believe strongly in the instructor-led class. During class, focus on your instructor. Our manuals are designed and written to facilitate your interaction with your instructor, and not to call attention to manuals themselves.

We believe in the basic approach of setting expectations, delivering instruction, and providing summary and review afterwards. For this reason, lessons begin with objectives and end with summaries. We also provide overall course objectives and a course summary to provide both an introduction to and closure on the entire course.

Manual components

The manuals contain these major components:

- Table of contents
- Introduction
- Units
- Course summary
- Glossary
- Index

Each element is described below.

Table of contents

The table of contents acts as a learning roadmap.

Introduction

The introduction contains information about our training philosophy and our manual components, features, and conventions. It contains target student, prerequisite, objective, and setup information for the specific course.

Units

Units are the largest structural component of the course content. A unit begins with a title page that lists objectives for each major subdivision, or topic, within the unit. Within each topic, conceptual and explanatory information alternates with hands-on activities. Units conclude with a summary comprising one paragraph for each topic, and an independent practice activity that gives you an opportunity to practice the skills you've learned.

The conceptual information takes the form of text paragraphs, exhibits, lists, and tables. The activities are structured in two columns, one telling you what to do, the other providing explanations, descriptions, and graphics.

Course summary

This section provides a text summary of the entire course. It is useful for providing closure at the end of the course. The course summary also indicates the next course in this series, if there is one, and lists additional resources you might find useful as you continue to learn about the software.

Glossary

The glossary provides definitions for all of the key terms used in this course.

Index

The index at the end of this manual makes it easy for you to find information about a particular software component, feature, or concept.

Manual conventions

We've tried to keep the number of elements and the types of formatting to a minimum in the manuals. This aids in clarity and makes the manuals more classically elegant looking. But there are some conventions and icons you should know about.

Item	Description
Italic text	In conceptual text, indicates a new term or feature.
Bold text	In unit summaries, indicates a key term or concept. In an independent practice activity, indicates an explicit item that you select, choose, or type.
`Code font`	Indicates code or syntax.

`Longer strings of ▶`
`code will look ▶`
`like this.`
	In the hands-on activities, any code that's too long to fit on a single line is divided into segments by one or more continuation characters (▶). This code should be entered as a continuous string of text.

Select **bold item**	In the left column of hands-on activities, bold sans-serif text indicates an explicit item that you select, choose, or type.
Keycaps like ↵ ENTER	Indicate a key on the keyboard you must press.

Hands-on activities

The hands-on activities are the most important parts of our manuals. They are divided into two primary columns. The "Here's how" column gives short instructions to you about what to do. The "Here's why" column provides explanations, graphics, and clarifications. Here's a sample:

Do it!

A-1: Creating a commission formula

Here's how	Here's why
1 Open Sales	This is an oversimplified sales compensation worksheet. It shows sales totals, commissions, and incentives for five sales reps.
2 Observe the contents of cell F4	F4 = =E4*C_Rate The commission rate formulas use the name "C_Rate" instead of a value for the commission rate.

For these activities, we have provided a collection of data files designed to help you learn each skill in a real-world business context. As you work through the activities, you will modify and update these files. Of course, you might make a mistake and therefore want to re-key the activity starting from scratch. To make it easy to start over, you will rename each data file at the end of the first activity in which the file is modified. Our convention for renaming files is to add the word "My" to the beginning of the file name. In the above activity, for example, a file called "Sales" is being used for the first time. At the end of this activity, you would save the file as "My sales," thus leaving the "Sales" file unchanged. If you make a mistake, you can start over using the original "Sales" file.

In some activities, however, it might not be practical to rename the data file. If you want to retry one of these activities, ask your instructor for a fresh copy of the original data file.

Topic B: Setting your expectations

Properly setting your expectations is essential to your success. This topic will help you do that by providing:

- Prerequisites for this course
- A description of the target student
- A list of the objectives for the course
- A skills assessment for the course

Course prerequisites

Students taking this course should be familiar with personal computers and the use of a keyboard and a mouse.

Target student

This course is designed for people with no working knowledge of Windows who need to learn how to use Windows 7. This course is an entry-level course for the Windows 7 end-user.

Course objectives

These overall course objectives will give you an idea about what to expect from the course. It is also possible that they will help you see that this course is not the right one for you. If you think you either lack the prerequisite knowledge or already know most of the subject matter to be covered, you should let your instructor know that you think you are misplaced in the class.

After completing this course, you will know how to:

- Log on to Windows 7 and identify the desktop components; open applications and switch between applications; move and resize windows; work with commands and dialog boxes; and find information in Windows Help and Support.
- Create and manage folders and libraries; and create and manage files.
- Customize Windows Explorer; edit file metadata; customize folders; and search the computer for specific content.
- Customize the desktop and Start menu; use Windows 7 gadgets; and configure system settings with the Control Panel.
- Browse the Web with Internet Explorer; use the tabbed browsing feature; search for content on the Web; customize Internet Explorer; and access multimedia content on the Web.

Skills inventory

Use the following form to gauge your skill level entering the class. For each skill listed, rate your familiarity from 1 to 5, with five being the most familiar. *This is not a test.* Rather, it is intended to provide you with an idea of where you're starting from at the beginning of class. If you're wholly unfamiliar with all the skills, you might not be ready for the class. If you think you already understand all of the skills, you might need to move on to the next course in the series. In either case, you should let your instructor know as soon as possible.

Skill	1	2	3	4	5
Logging onto Windows 7					
Using the Start menu to open applications					
Moving and resizing an application window					
Using menus, toolbars, and scrollbars					
Using the Windows 7 Help and Support feature					
Opening Documents, Pictures, and other libraries					
Browsing the file hierarchy in Windows Explorer					
Adding and removing gadgets					
Opening files in the Documents folder					
Creating text files					
Creating and renaming folders					
Moving and copying files and folders					
Searching for content in folders					
Adding and removing icons on the taskbar and Start menu					
Changing system settings for the mouse and keyboard					
Changing the desktop background and screen saver					
Browsing the Web with Internet Explorer					
Working with Favorites, RSS feeds, and the History list					
Using tabs in Internet Explorer					
Playing multimedia content in Windows Media Player and Internet Explorer					

Topic C: Re-keying the course

If you have the proper hardware and software, you can re-key this course after class. This section explains what you'll need in order to do so, and how to do it.

Hardware requirements

Your personal computer should have:

- 1 GHz or faster 32- or 64-bit processor
- At least 1 GB of RAM
- At least 16 GB hard-disk space, 40 GB or more recommended
- Video adapter card compatible with DirectX 9 or newer, with at least 64 MB video memory
- A keyboard and a mouse
- Printer (useful but not required)
- DVD drive if you'll be installing via disc

Software requirements

You will need the following software:

- Windows 7 Professional or Ultimate

Network requirements

The following network components and connectivity are also required for this course:

- Local network access if you want to access data files over a network
- Internet access, for the following purposes:
  - Downloading the latest critical updates and service packs from www.windowsupdate.com
  - Downloading the Student Data files from www.axzopress.com (if necessary)
  - Completing activities in the unit titled "Internet Explorer 8"

Setup instructions to re-key the course

Before you re-key the course, you will need to perform the following steps. You will need administrator level access to your computer to complete these steps.

1 Install Windows 7 according to the software manufacturer's instructions.

Enter a user name of **User01** and computer name of **Comp01**. Set the password to **p@ssword**. Set a password hint of your choice.

Use the recommended settings for updates. When you are prompted for the location of your network, choose Work.

If you do not install antivirus software, Windows will warn you that your computer might be at risk.

2 If you don't have the data CD that came with this manual, download the Student Data files for the course. You can download the data directly to student machines, to a central location on your own network, or to a disk.

a Connect to www.axzopress.com.

b Under Downloads, click Instructor-Led Training.

c Browse the subject categories to locate your course. Then click the course title to display a list of available downloads. (You can also access these downloads through our Catalog listings.)

d Click the link(s) for downloading the Student Data files, and follow the instructions that appear on your screen.

3 If the data file is an executable compressed file, it will create a Student Data folder and copy the files to it. If not, create a folder named **Student Data** on the C: drive and copy the data files to it.

4 Open C:\Student Data\Unit 2\ and move the files from "Move to My Documents" to your My Documents folder. Move the files from "Move to My Pictures" to your My Pictures folder. Move the files but not the folders, and delete the empty folders when you're done. Leave any other folders as they are.

Repeat this step for Units 3 and 4. The files to be moved in Units 3 and 4 are the same as those for Unit 2, so if you are keying the entire course, you might not need to move them, but you should still delete the folders Move to My Documents and Move to My Pictures. Again, leave any other folders.

5 Open Internet Explorer to answer questions about setup. Don't turn on Suggested sites. Use Express settings to finish the setup. Set the Home page to Google; it's simple and loads quickly. Close Internet Explorer.

6 Log off.

CertBlaster pre- and post-assessment software

CertBlaster pre- and post-assessment software is available for this course. To download and install this free software, complete the following steps:

1. Go to www.axzopress.com.
2. Under Downloads, click CertBlaster.
3. Click the link for Windows 7.
4. Save the .EXE file to a folder on your hard drive. (**Note:** If you skip this step, the CertBlaster software will not install correctly.)
5. Click Start and choose Run.
6. Click Browse and then navigate to the folder that contains the .EXE file.
7. Select the .EXE file and click Open.
8. Click OK and follow the on-screen instructions. When prompted for the password, enter **c_Win7**.

Unit 1

The Windows 7 environment

Unit time: 90 minutes

Complete this unit, and you'll know how to:

A Log on to Windows 7 and identify the desktop components.

B Use the Start button to open applications, and use the taskbar to switch between applications.

C Move and resize windows, work with commands, and use dialog boxes.

D Use Windows Help and Support to find information and solutions to problems, and log off of Windows.

Topic A: The Windows 7 desktop

Explanation

Windows 7 is an operating system. An *operating system* is software you use to interact with the computer's hardware components, such as the mouse, the keyboard, and the computer's memory. Your computer must have an operating system installed before it can perform any other operations. The operating system automatically starts when you switch on the computer. The startup process is called *booting*.

In most work and school environments, computers with Windows (including previous versions of Windows) are connected to each other to form a *network*. Computers on a network can share resources such as files and printers.

Logging on

Windows 7 provides built-in security measures to ensure that only authorized users can access the computer. To access most Windows 7 computers, you will need a user name and a password, which you will type in a procedure known as *logging on*. The entire process of verifying who you are and granting you access is known as the *logon process*. This process helps protect your documents from unauthorized users.

To log on to your computer:

1 Start your computer. Windows 7 displays the logon screen.
2 Click the applicable user name. If there is only one user on a computer, you will not see a list to choose from.
3 If prompted, enter your password, and press Enter or click the arrow.

If the computer is set up with only one user and no password, Windows will not stop at the logon screen, but will continue to load the desktop.

Do it!

A-1: Logging on to a Windows 7 computer

Here's how	Here's why
1 Observe the logon screen	To see the available user accounts and the option to log on by using an account that's not listed.
2 Click **User##**	Where ## is your computer number. Your user name was created during the installation and setup of Windows 7 for this class. Ask your instructor if you're not sure which user account is yours.
3 Type **p@ssword**	To enter the password.
4 Press ↵ ENTER	To log on to the computer and display the Windows desktop.

Desktop components

Explanation

After you log on, the Windows 7 *desktop* appears. Just as a physical desk holds the tools you need to do your work, the Windows 7 desktop provides access to *programs* (also called *applications*), which you can use to perform such tasks as creating, editing, and printing documents. Exhibit 1-1 shows an example of the Windows 7 desktop.

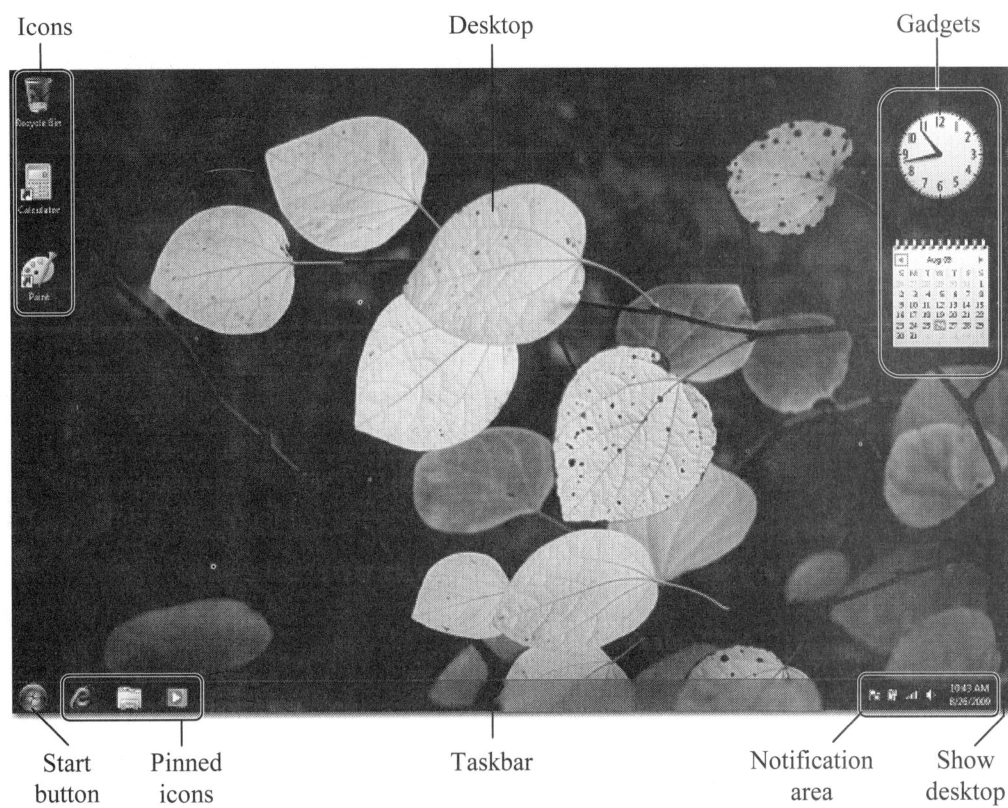

Exhibit 1-1: Windows 7 desktop components

The following table describes some of the major desktop components.

Component	Description
Background	The background is a color or image that fills the screen and extends behind the other desktop elements. You can customize your desktop background.
Icons and shortcuts	An *icon* is a small pictorial representation of a program, command, or data file on the computer. Double-clicking a desktop icon opens it. By default, the desktop contains an icon for the Recycle Bin. A *shortcut* is an icon that is a link to a file, folder, or program that resides elsewhere on the computer (not on the desktop). A shortcut has a small curved arrow in the corner of the icon.
Gadgets	Gadgets are small programs that usually perform a single, simple function. Examples include a clock, a calculator, news feeds, and small games and slide shows.
Taskbar	The taskbar is a rectangular bar that contains the Start button, pinned icons and open-program icons (next to the Start button), the notification area (where the clock is located), and the Show Desktop button.
Start button	You can use the Start button to open applications and to access any resource or feature on the computer.
Pinned icons	These are icons for commonly used programs. You open them with a single click, rather than the double-click used for desktop icons. Other programs that are open will have icons to the right of the pinned icons.
Notification area (system tray)	The area contains the date and time, as well as any icons showing the status of background programs. The sound volume control is here.
Show Desktop	This is a small rectangular button at the far end of the taskbar. Holding the mouse pointer over the Show Desktop button will make open windows look transparent. Clicking the button will minimize all windows so you can see the entire desktop.

Windows Aero and system resources

As with Windows Vista, using the more advanced interface features of Windows 7 requires a computer with better graphics capabilities. If a system does not have sufficient resources, many of the Windows Aero features—like Aero Peek and Flip 3-D, which will be discussed later—will not be available. Instead, you'll see simpler, opaque versions of these features. You can also opt to turn these features off if you think they are slowing down your computer.

Do it!

A-2: Identifying desktop components

Here's how	Here's why
1 Observe the desktop	You're going to get acquainted with the Windows 7 desktop.
2 Observe the Recycle Bin icon	Recycle Bin The Recycle Bin is your computer's trash can. Deleted items are stored here until you empty the trash. If you change your mind and want to keep some items you have deleted, you can retrieve them from the Recycle Bin before you empty it.
3 Observe the taskbar	(At the bottom of the screen.) You can use the taskbar to navigate in Windows 7. The taskbar contains the Start button and the notification area. Pinned icons for common tasks appear to the right of the Start button.
4 Observe the Start button	(On the taskbar.) You can use this button to start just about any activity on your computer, including opening applications, getting help, configuring your computer, searching for items on your computer, and shutting down your computer.
5 Observe the pinned icons	(To the right of the Start button.) These represent commonly used programs. You decide what programs go here. By default, there are pinned icons for Internet Explorer, Windows Explorer, and Windows Media Player.
6 Observe the notification area	(On the right side of the taskbar.) It contains a clock that displays the current time, and it might contain icons for some programs or other options on your computer.
7 Observe the clock	(In the notification area.) It displays the current time. To the right of this is a small rectangle you can click to show the desktop.

The mouse and mouse pointer

Explanation

The *mouse* is an input device you can use to perform various tasks such as opening applications, selecting items, copying data, and moving data. The mouse moves on a flat surface, usually a *mouse pad.* As you move the mouse, a *mouse pointer*—an icon that changes shape depending on its location or current function—moves in the same direction on the screen.

Exhibit 1-2: The Recycle Bin icon, showing a ToolTip

By default, the left mouse button is the *primary* mouse button. You use the primary mouse button for selecting, moving, and opening objects. You can configure the right mouse button as the primary mouse button if that would be more comfortable for you.

The following table describes the mouse actions and how to perform them, with the left mouse button serving as the primary button.

Action	What you do
Point	Place the mouse pointer over an object.
Click	Press and release the primary mouse button.
Double-click	Press and release the primary mouse button two times in rapid succession.
Drag and drop	Point to an item, hold down the primary mouse button, move the pointer to another location, and then release the mouse button. This process is also called *dragging;* usually, an instruction to drag an object implies dropping it, too.
Right-click	Press and release the secondary (typically the right) mouse button.

Windows ToolTips

Windows 7 provides a helpful feature called *ToolTips*. ToolTips are information boxes that appear when you hold the mouse pointer over desktop icons and toolbar buttons for a few seconds.

Do it!

A-3: Using the mouse

Here's how	Here's why
1 Observe the arrow on the desktop	This arrow is referred to as the *mouse pointer*, or simply the *pointer*. You can use it for various activities such as selecting an icon on the desktop or opening an application.
2 Move the mouse	The movement of the pointer on the desktop corresponds to the movement of the mouse.
3 Place the pointer over the Recycle Bin icon	This is called *pointing to* an icon. After a few seconds, Windows 7 displays a message called a ToolTip, as shown in Exhibit 1-2. The ToolTip describes the object's function.
4 While pointing to the Recycle Bin, click the left mouse button	(Press and release the left mouse button.) This action is called *selecting* an object.
Observe the icon	The icon appears highlighted. This indicates that it is selected.
5 Right-click **Recycle Bin**	Point to the Recycle Bin and click the right mouse button. A menu—a list of commands—appears.
Observe the menu	**Open** Empty Recycle Bin Create shortcut Rename Properties This shortcut menu contains frequently used commands related to the Recycle Bin. If there's nothing in the bin, the Empty option will be grayed out.
Click anywhere on a blank area of the desktop	To close the shortcut menu.
6 Point to the Recycle Bin icon	You'll move the icon.
Press and hold down the mouse button while moving the pointer to the center of the screen	This action is called *dragging* an icon. The shadow of the icon moves along with the pointer.
Release the button	This action is called *dropping*. Generally, if an instruction says to drag an object, the dropping is implied.
Observe the desktop	The Recycle Bin icon has been moved to the new location.

Topic B: The taskbar

Explanation

The taskbar contains the Start button, program icons, and the notification area. The taskbar has changed in both behavior and appearance from previous versions of Windows. By default, the taskbar is at the bottom of the desktop, but you can move it to any edge. You can use the Start button to open applications and to access any resource on the computer. To the right of the Start button are "pinned" icons, used to launch your most commonly used programs.

The Start menu

You can use the Start menu, shown in Exhibit 1-3, to open applications, get help, configure your computer, search for files on your computer, and shut down your computer. When you click the Start button (the round button at the left end of the taskbar), the Start menu appears. You can also open the Start menu by pressing Ctrl+Esc or the Windows logo key.

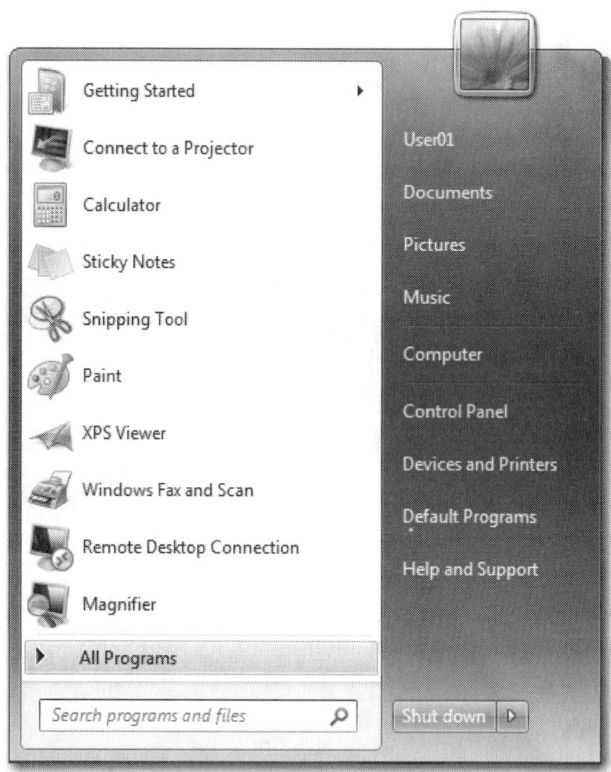

Exhibit 1-3: The Start menu

The Start menu is divided into two panes. The left pane contains commands for opening the most frequently used applications. (When you first install Windows, default programs are listed here.) You can "pin" programs that you use often to the Start menu—just right-click the program icon and choose Pin to Start Menu. You can click All Programs to navigate to any program on your computer. At the bottom of the left pane, there's a text box you can use to search for files and folders on your computer.

The name of the user who is currently logged on appears (with the account icon) at the top of the right pane of the Start menu. The right pane provides access to various folders, such as your Documents, Pictures, and Music folders. You can also open the Control Panel and Windows Help and Support from here. At the bottom of the right pane is the Shut down command, which provides access to commands for locking the computer and shutting it down.

Taskbar icons

To the right of the Start button are large, pinned icons for frequently used programs. Click one of these icons once to open the corresponding program. When the program is open, its taskbar button will appear highlighted, as shown in Exhibit 1-4. If you open a program from the Start menu, an icon will appear to the right of the pinned icons. If you open multiple instances of a program or open two documents in the same program (e.g., two WordPad documents at the same time), the corresponding icon will look as if several icons have been stacked atop each other.

Unpinned icons appear on the taskbar in the order in which you open the programs, but you can drag them to change their order. Icons for open programs look the same whether they are pinned or not—you can't tell if an open icon is pinned by looking at it. The icon for the active program, however, is lighter than the others.

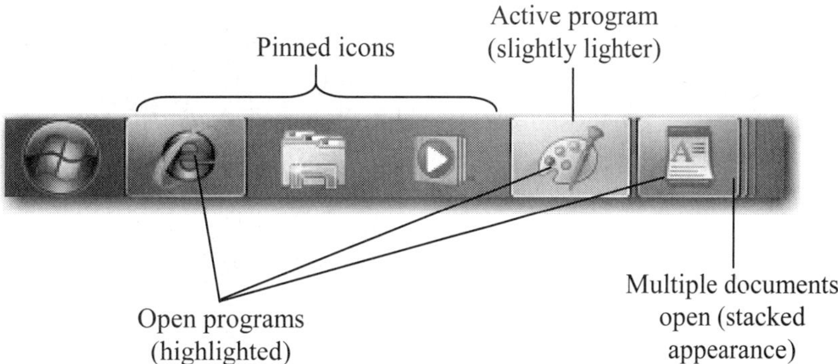

Exhibit 1-4: Taskbar icons

Do it!

B-1: Using the Start menu

Here's how	Here's why
1 Point to [Start button]	(This is the Start button.) A ToolTip appears after a moment. You're going to explore the Start menu in this activity.
2 Click the **Start** button	To display the Start menu. The Start menu is divided into two panes.
3 Observe the All Programs command	▶ **All Programs** The triangle indicates that this command opens a submenu.
4 Click **All Programs**	The All Programs submenu appears, displaying commands for opening folders and applications.
5 Click **Accessories**	To expand Accessories and display the items it contains.
6 Click **Notepad**	To open the Notepad application. The Document – Notepad window is displayed.
7 Observe the title bar	(On the top of the Notepad window.) The title bar displays the name of the open file (Untitled) and the name of the application (Notepad).
8 Observe the taskbar	It contains an icon for the Notepad application.
9 Open WordPad	Choose Start, All Programs, Accessories, WordPad.
10 Click **Start** and choose **Calculator**	To open the Calculator application.
Observe the taskbar	The taskbar icon for the Windows Calculator application is highlighted to indicate that it's the active application. The Notepad icon is still there, indicating that the Notepad application is open but not active (a state also known as "running in the background").
11 Open **Paint**	Click Start and choose All Programs, Accessories, Paint.

12 Click the taskbar icon for Internet Explorer	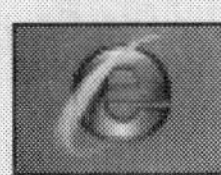 To open Internet Explorer, which is a Web browsing application. Windows does not add another program icon to the taskbar; it just highlights the pinned Internet Explorer icon that's already there.
13 In Internet Explorer, click the little blank tab, as shown	 A new tab opens. The taskbar icon for Internet Explorer now has a stacked appearance.

Switching between open files and programs

Explanation

When you're working with various open files and programs, you'll probably need to switch back and forth between those open items. In Windows 7, you can use Aero Peek, Flip, or Flip 3-D to quickly switch between open files and programs.

Aero Peek

Pointing to the icon for a running program will show you a "live thumbnail"—a small picture—of that program window, even if it's hidden from view on the desktop. A live thumbnail reflects what's happening in the window, so if a video is playing or a progress bar is showing a download, you'll see these things moving in the thumbnail.

Pointing to a thumbnail will make all other windows transparent so that you can see the corresponding program window at full size. Microsoft calls this feature *Aero Peek*. If you click the thumbnail, you will switch to that program window.

You can close a window by clicking the Close button on the corresponding thumbnail. You can also use Aero Peek to show the whole desktop.

The Show Desktop button

The Show Desktop icon in previous Windows versions has been replaced by a small rectangle at the right end of the taskbar. If you hold the mouse pointer over this rectangle, all open windows become transparent, and you can see the desktop. Click the button, and all windows will be minimized.

Windows Flip and Flip 3-D

You can flip through open applications and the desktop by pressing Alt+Tab. This key combination displays thumbnails of all open programs, as shown in the top picture in Exhibit 1-5. You can switch applications by pressing Tab while you hold down the Alt key. You can hold down the Windows key and press Tab to flip through 3-D versions of the open windows, as shown in the bottom picture in Exhibit 1-5.

Exhibit 1-5: Windows Flip (top) and Flip 3-D (bottom)

Do it!

B-2: Switching between applications

Here's how	Here's why
1 Verify that Internet Explorer is active	
2 On the taskbar, hold the mouse pointer over the Calculator icon	After a couple seconds, a thumbnail of the calculator appears.
Hold the mouse pointer over the thumbnail calculator	After a few seconds, the other windows go transparent, showing only the calculator on the desktop and outlines of the other windows.
3 Click the thumbnail calculator	To activate Calculator.

4 On the taskbar, point to the Internet Explorer icon	Both browser tabs appear as thumbnails.
Point to one Internet Explorer thumbnail, and then the other	(Don't click either one; just point.) The view switches between the two.
5 Move the pointer away from the taskbar	Calculator is still the active program because you did not click any thumbnails.
6 Right-click the Internet Explorer icon and choose **Close Window**	A dialog box asks you if you want to close all tabs or just the current one.
Click **Close all tabs**	To close Internet Explorer.
7 Click the WordPad icon	(Don't wait for the thumbnails to appear.) WordPad becomes active immediately.
8 Press and hold ALT, and press TAB several times	All the thumbnails appear in a row across the screen, and different programs are highlighted as you press Tab.
9 Release ALT, and press and hold the Windows key	If your keyboard has one.
Press TAB several times	To flip through the windows in 3-D, even if some or all windows are minimized.
Stop at the Paint program	(Release the Windows and Tab keys.) To leave this program active.
10 Point to the Show Desktop button	(The small rectangle at the far right end of the taskbar.) After a second, all windows become transparent.
Move the pointer away	The windows reappear.
11 Click the Show Desktop button	All windows are minimized.
Click it again	All windows are restored.

Topic C: Window management

Explanation

Almost all of your work in Windows 7 takes place in one window or another. A *window* is a movable, sizable area that displays information. Each running application has its own window and might even display more than one window.

Windows differ from dialog boxes, icons, buttons, and other user interface elements in a number of ways. Each of these elements is covered separately in this unit.

Window components

Most Windows 7 program windows contain the same basic components, though the layout can vary. Most windows have a title bar that displays the program name and the document name. Even though the purpose of each window differs, the basic components function the same way, so when you become familiar with the components, you'll be able to perform basic functions in just about any window.

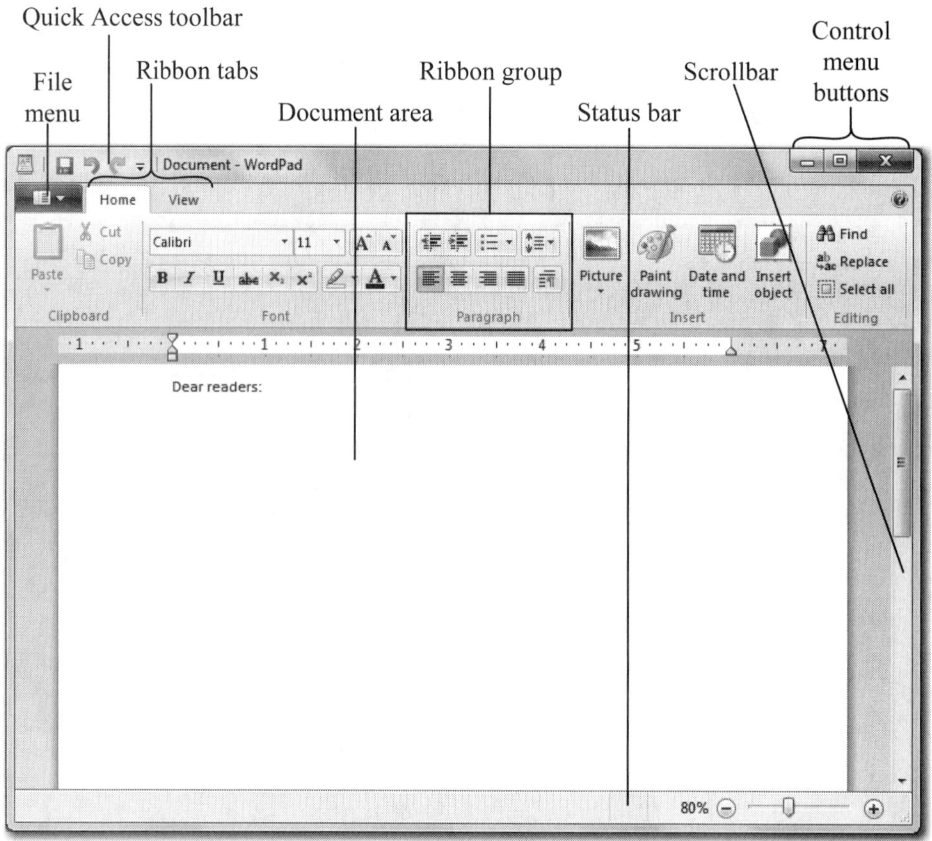

Exhibit 1-6: WordPad in Windows 7 uses a Ribbon

Toolbars and Ribbons

For many years, most programs had a menu bar and a toolbar under the title bar. More recently, due to larger screens and higher resolutions, many programs started using larger command ribbons or control panels, which lay out available commands more openly. Exhibit 1-6 shows Windows 7 WordPad, which uses a Ribbon.

The following table describes common window components.

Component	Description
Title bar	The horizontal bar located at the top of the window. The title bar displays the name of the application with which the window is associated. It often also shows the name of the active document.
Menu bar	The horizontal bar located below the title bar. It contains the menu commands for that program. Some programs have a Ribbon instead of a menu bar and toolbars.
Toolbar	A collection of buttons arranged on a bar below the title bar. You use these buttons to execute frequently used commands. Some applications call this bar the "button bar," "speed bar," "quick bar," and so forth.
Command ribbon or control panel	Typically a combination of menu bars and toolbars, which tend to lay out commands in a clear, graphical way (see Exhibit 1-6). Applications in the Microsoft Office 2007 suite use a Ribbon.
Status bar	The horizontal bar located at the bottom of the window. It provides information about the window and document and displays the status of various toggle keys (Caps Lock, Num Lock) on your keyboard. Not all windows display a status bar.
Control menu	A button, in the upper-left corner of a window, that displays a menu. Use this menu to expand a window so it covers the entire desktop area (maximize it), reduce a window to a taskbar button (minimize it), and close a window. The Control menu button takes on the appearance of each window's associated application icon.
Control menu buttons	A group of three buttons located in the upper-right corner of a window. Use these buttons to minimize, maximize, restore, or close a window.
Scrollbars	Bars on the right side and/or bottom of a window. Use them to scroll down in a document (or across it) if it is too long (or wide) to be shown in the window.

Moving and resizing windows

At some point you'll want to move or resize a window so you can better organize your desktop.

- To move a window, just drag its title bar to a new location.
- To resize a window, you drag an edge or a corner of it in the direction you want. (Hold the mouse pointer over an edge or corner of the window. When the pointer turns into a double-headed arrow, you can drag to resize.)

You cannot move or resize a maximized window because it already fills the entire desktop. Also, some applications, like the Calculator, are not resizable.

Aero Snap and Shake

The Snap and Shake features are new in Windows 7. Here's how to use the Snap feature to quickly resize windows:

- To maximize a window, drag its title bar up until the pointer hits the top of the screen. To restore the window to its former size, drag it down.
- To resize a window so it takes up half of the desktop, drag the window's title bar to the left or right until the pointer hits the edge of the screen. A quick way to compare two windows is to drag one to the left side and one to the right. To restore the window to its former size, drag it away from the edge of the screen.
- To resize a window so it uses the full height of the screen, but without changing the width, drag the window's bottom edge down to the bottom of the screen.

If you have multiple windows open and you want to quickly minimize all but one window, you can use the Shake feature. To do so, you "shake" the desired window by dragging the title bar back and forth quickly. Shake it again to restore all the other windows.

Do it!

C-1: Moving and resizing windows

Here's how	Here's why
1 Activate WordPad	Click its taskbar icon. You don't have to click the thumbnail because only one instance is open.
2 Point to the middle of the title bar	
3 Drag the window left or right	To move the window around.
4 Activate Notepad	You'll change the size of this window.
5 Point to the top edge of the window	The shape of the pointer changes to a vertical double-headed arrow.
6 Drag the edge upward	To expand the window in the direction you drag in.
Observe the window	The height of the window has increased.
7 Point to the left edge of the window	The pointer changes to a horizontal double-headed arrow.
Drag the edge to the right	To reduce the width of the window, moving its left edge in the direction you drag.
Observe the window	The width of the window has decreased.
8 Decrease the height of the window	Point to the bottom edge of the window and drag upward, or drag the top edge downward.
9 Point to the lower-right corner of the window	The pointer changes to a diagonal double-headed arrow.
Drag the corner diagonally downward and to the right	To increase the height and width of the window simultaneously.

10 Decrease both the height and width of the window	Drag the lower-right corner of the window diagonally upward and to the left.
11 Drag the window's title bar to the very top of the desktop	(Don't resize the window; just drag the title bar as you would to move the window.) When the pointer reaches the top edge of the screen, the window maximizes. This is one example of the Snap feature.
12 Drag the title bar down	The window is restored to its previous size.
13 Drag the title bar to the right until the pointer reaches the edge of the desktop	When the pointer reaches the right side of the screen, the window "snaps" to the right side, filling up the right half of the screen. You can use this method to quickly view documents or other items side by side.
14 Use the Snap feature to have the Paint window take up the left half of the screen	Drag the Paint window's title bar to the left until the pointer reaches the edge of the desktop.
15 Drag the title bars of both windows down	To restore the Paint and Notepad windows to their previous sizes.
Move and resize the Paint and Notepad windows so they do not go off the desktop	If necessary.

The Control menu and buttons

Explanation

The Control menu is in the upper-left corner of the Window. It often has an icon that represents the application. Control menu buttons appear in the upper-right corner of a window (on the title bar). You can use the Control menu and the buttons to maximize, minimize, restore, or close a window.

Button	Name	Description
	Minimize	Minimizes the window to the taskbar button.
	Maximize	Enlarges the window to cover the entire desktop. A window will have either the Maximize button or the Restore Down button, depending on its current state.
	Restore Down	Restores the window to its previous size.
X	Close	Closes the application.

Do it!

C-2: Using the Control menu buttons

Here's how	Here's why
1 Activate Paint	(If necessary.) You'll use the Control menu buttons to maximize, restore, minimize, and close the window.
2 Click	(The Maximize button.) To maximize the window. The window now covers the entire desktop, except the taskbar.
Observe the middle Control menu button	The Maximize button has been replaced by the Restore Down button.
3 Click	To restore the window to its previous size. The Maximize button now appears as the middle Control menu button.
4 Click	To minimize the window to a taskbar button.
5 Click the Calculator taskbar icon	To activate the Calculator.
Observe the Control menu buttons	The Maximize button is grayed out. You can't use it because calculator cannot be resized (though it can be minimized),
6 Click X	(The Close button.) To close the Calculator application.

Using commands

Explanation

A *menu* is a list of commands that you can use to accomplish specific tasks. The menu bar contains a series of menus, which in turn contain commands. Some commands open additional menus, called *submenus*. When you click an item on the menu bar, the corresponding menu appears; for example, click File to display a menu of file-related commands. Choose a command to accomplish a certain task, such as opening or saving a file. Exhibit 1-7 shows the Format menu, with the Paragraph command highlighted.

Toolbars contain buttons that provide access to frequently used commands. You will find that most of these commands are also available on the menus. You can perform a task quickly by clicking its toolbar button. Toolbars are typically below the menu bar.

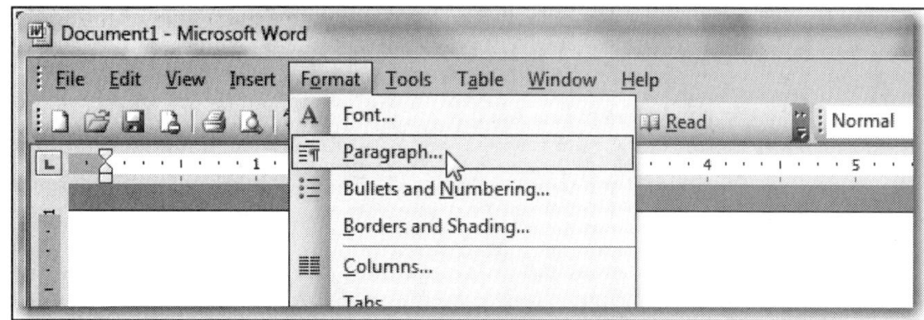

Exhibit 1-7: The menu bar and toolbar in Word 2003

Ribbons

A *Ribbon* (sometimes called a control panel in other applications) is a combination of menu bar and toolbar, and shows commands in a clear, graphical way. Ribbons typically have several tabs for different categories of commands, and the tabs are divided into groups. In Exhibit 1-8, the Ribbon tabs in Word 2007 are labeled Home, Insert, Page Layout, and so on, while the Ribbon groups on the Home tab are labeled Clipboard, Font, and Paragraph (among others not shown). As you can see, the program groups correspond to the menu items in the earlier version of Word.

Even programs with Ribbon interfaces will usually have quick-access buttons and the equivalent of a File menu for common tasks like opening, saving, and printing documents.

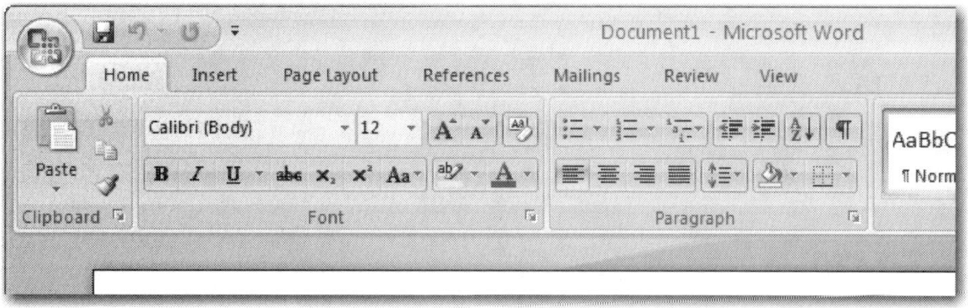

Exhibit 1-8: The command Ribbon in Word 2007

Do it!

C-3: Working with commands

Here's how	Here's why
1 Activate Notepad	If necessary.

Step	Action	Result
2	Observe the menu bar	(Below the title bar.) It contains several menus.
3	Click **File**	(On the menu bar.) To display the File menu.
	Observe the File menu	Any dimmed commands indicate that they are not currently available.
4	Point to **Edit**	To display the Edit menu.
5	View the commands available on the remaining Notepad menus	Each menu offers a different set of commands.
6	Click the title bar, or click in a blank area of the Notepad window	To close the menu. You can also press the Esc key.
7	Activate Paint	You'll work with the Ribbon.
8	Observe the Ribbon	The Home tab is active, showing many of the most common tasks.
9	On the Ribbon, click the **View** tab	To display the commands for changing the view.
10	Click the button to the left of the Home tab label, as shown	Home Cut To display a menu that has commands that used to be on the File menu, plus some others.
11	Click the button again	To close the menu.

Scrolling

Explanation

Scrollbars appear in a window when it contains information that extends beyond the current borders of the window. Using the vertical scrollbar, you can adjust the view up and down; using the horizontal scrollbar, you can adjust the view to the left or right.

Do it!

C-4: Using scrollbars

Here's how	Here's why
1 Right-click a blank area of the desktop and choose **Personalize**	You'll work with a scrollbar.
2 Click the link for **Desktop Background**	At the bottom of the window.
3 Observe the pictures pane	(In the middle.) It contains a scrollbar so you can scroll through the pictures. Your current background is shown with a checkmark.
4 Point to the scroll box and drag it upward slowly	
Observe the pictures	You're scrolling up through the available desktop backgrounds.
5 At the top of the scrollbar, click ▲	(The scroll-up arrow is on the scrollbar.) To scroll up.
Observe the scrollbar	The scroll box moved up.
6 In the Events pane, click ▼	(The scroll-down arrow is on the scrollbar.) To scroll down.
Observe the scrollbar	The scroll box moved down.
7 Close the Personalize window	Click the Close button in the upper-right corner of the window.

Dialog boxes

Explanation

Dialog boxes are special types of windows that appear when you choose certain menu commands or click certain command buttons. You use dialog boxes to enter the specific information that is required to complete a task. For example, when you save a file for the first time, you use the Save As dialog box to enter a name for the file and specify the location where you want to save the file.

The following table describes the objects you'll find in dialog boxes.

Object	Description
Text box	A box into which you enter text.
Command buttons	Buttons you click to initiate or confirm an action.
Checkboxes	Boxes you use to specify on/off or yes/no selections from a set of non-exclusive options. A checkmark will appear in a checkbox to indicate that the option has been selected.
Radio buttons	Buttons you use to specify on/off or yes/no selections from a set of exclusive options. In other words, only one option can be chosen in a set of radio buttons. The radio button will be filled in with a dot to indicate that the option has been selected.
List box	A list of items from which you can select individual items.
Drop-down list box	A special form of list box that shows just one of the possible options. To select one of the other options, you first click an arrow to display the full list.

The Save As dialog box

When creating documents, you will want to save your work. The first time you save a document, you will use the Save As dialog box, shown in Exhibit 1-9, to give your document a name and tell Windows 7 where to store it. You'll see files of the same type as the one you are saving. Save As dialog boxes can look a little different from one program to another, but they usually have the same elements.

Often, you will edit a document and then save it with the same name at the same location. This action is called an *update save* and does not require you to use the Save As dialog box.

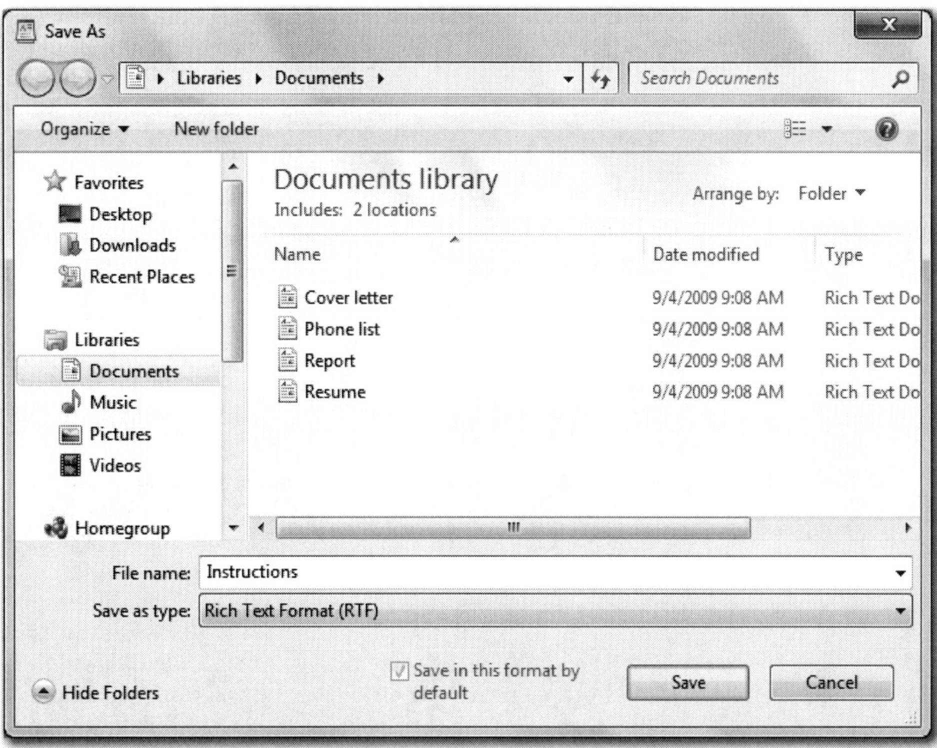

Exhibit 1-9: The Save As dialog box

Do it!

C-5: Using the Save As dialog box

Here's how	Here's why
1 Activate Notepad	You'll work with the Save As dialog box in Notepad.
2 Type **Salt and pepper**	The text appears in the Notepad window.
3 Choose **File**, **Save As...**	To open the Save As dialog box. Because you haven't saved this document yet, you need to tell Windows where to save it and what to name it. The dialog box prompts you to specify the desired name and location. The insertion point is in the File name box.
4 Observe the Address bar	It shows that you are in the Documents library. You'll save your document in your own Documents folder.
5 Type **Ingredients list**	(In the File name box.) To name the document. If the .txt extension is already there, don't worry about replacing it.
6 Click **Save**	The Save button tells Windows 7 to save the document with the specified name.
7 Close Notepad	
8 Close all open windows	

Topic D: Windows Help and Support

Explanation

Learning Windows can sometimes seem like a difficult task. Microsoft provides you with various tools to help you find important information or solve specific problems. The Windows Help and Support system provides many ways for you to find help, including:

- Listing detailed steps for completing procedures
- Defining terms
- Listing topics related to your particular Help request
- Providing links to common support tasks, such as using Windows Update (where you get updates to Windows 7)
- Providing search options to help you get more precise information

As shown in Exhibit 1-10, Windows Help and Support provides a toolbar and a Search box near the top of the window. There are also links to current Microsoft information from Windows Online Help and Support. The main window is divided into common questions and links for finding help on the Web.

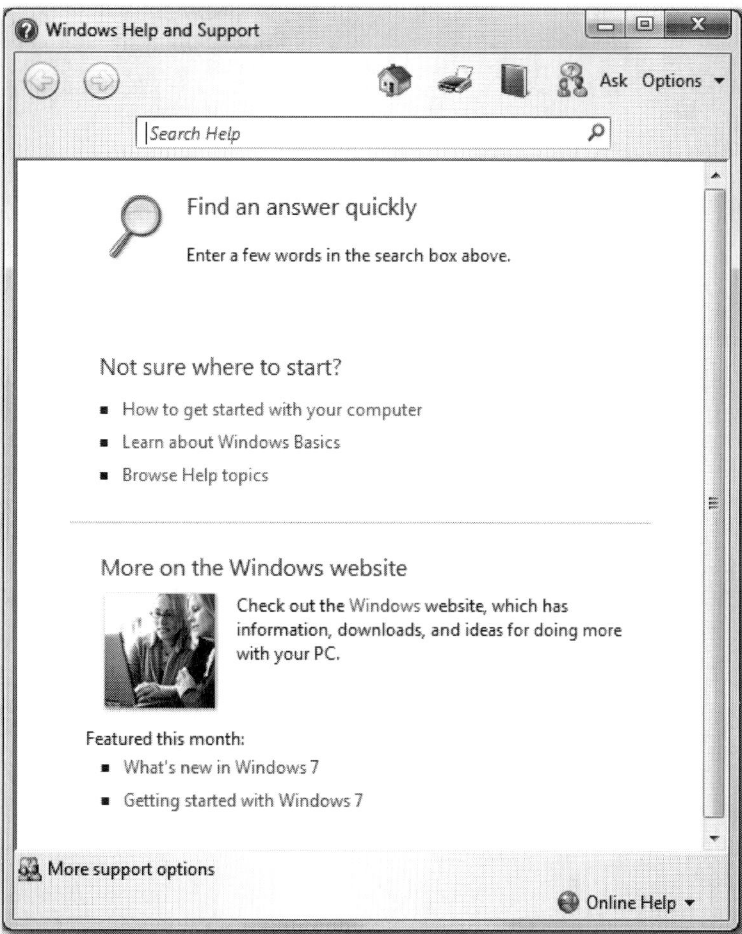

Exhibit 1-10: Windows Help and Support

The Windows Help and Support toolbar

The Help toolbar, located below the title bar, makes it easy to work with Windows Help and Support and to find your way through various Help topics. For example, if you want to return to the previously displayed topic, click the Back button on the toolbar. The following table describes the buttons on the Help toolbar.

Button	Description
	Returns you to the previous Help topic.
	Moves forward to the next Help topic. This button is available only after you click the Back button.
	Quickly returns you to the main Help and Support Center window.
	Enables you to print a Help topic.
	Provides a list of Help topics.
 Ask	Provides access to Remote Assistance and Windows communities (newsgroups) and other interactive assistance.
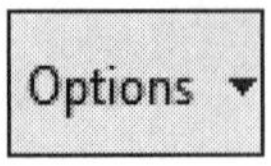 Options	Enables you to customize Windows Help and Support.

Do it!

D-1: Picking a Help topic

Here's how	Here's why
1 Click **Start** and choose **Help and Support**	To open Windows Help and Support. Microsoft has tried to anticipate the types of topics and tasks that you might need help with.
If prompted, click **Yes**	To get the latest help content from online.
2 Observe the toolbar	These buttons make it easy for you to move through the help system and access and print the information you need.
3 Under "Not sure where to start?" click **Learn about Windows Basics**	
4 Observe the help information	There are many basic topics to get you started.
5 Click	To return to the main page.
6 Click	To return to the topic you selected.
7 Click	To see a detailed table of contents.
8 Click a link in the list	To display another help topic.
9 Click	To return to the Windows Help and Support home page.
10 Click Ask	To display options for using Remote Assistance and accessing Windows newsgroups.
11 Click	
12 Click Options	To display additional features, available on the Options menu.
Press ESC	To close the menu.

Help search features

Explanation

You can use the Search feature in Windows Help and Support to look for information by using a single keyword, multiple keywords, or a complete phrase. After you enter the keywords, Windows scans the entire text of all Help documents for the keywords you entered. It then displays a list of all documents that contain at least one occurrence of those keywords.

Do it!

D-2: Searching for Help topics

Here's how	Here's why
1 In the Search box, type **taskbar**	(In Windows Help and Support.) You will search for all topics in which "taskbar" occurs at least once.
2 Press ENTER	Windows begins searching and displays a list of suggested topics.
3 Click **The taskbar (overview)**	To display information about the taskbar.
4 Click **Options** and choose **Find (on this page)...**	To open the Find dialog box.
5 Enter **minimize**	As you type, matching words are highlighted in the Help window behind the dialog box.
6 Drag the Find dialog box to one side	So you can see the whole Help window.
7 In the Find dialog box, click **Next**	To move to the next matching word.
Click **Next** a few more times	To see other instances of the word in this topic.
8 Click [X]	To close the Find dialog box.
9 Close Windows Help and Support	

Workstation security

Explanation

When you aren't using your computer, or if you have to leave your desk for any reason, you should make sure your workstation is secure. You don't want to leave your Windows 7 computer logged in with your user account, because anybody could sit down and access your files or your company's files on the network, send e-mail in your name, or perform other malicious or illegal acts.

To prevent this type of security breach, you should do one of the following:

- **Log off** — When you log off, Windows 7 saves any unsaved data and closes all programs.
- **Lock the computer** — When you lock the computer, your data is not saved to a disk drive, and your applications remain open. However, other users cannot access your data. You unlock the computer by entering your password.

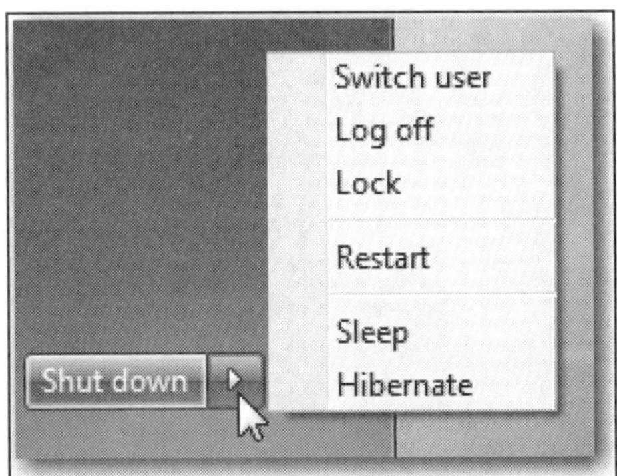

Exhibit 1-11: Shutdown and logoff options

To log off, click Start, click the arrow next to Shut down, as shown in Exhibit 1-11, and choose Log off.

To lock the workstation, click Start, click the arrow next to Shut down, and choose Lock. You can also hold down the Windows key and press L. To use the computer again, you will need to unlock it by entering your password.

Do it!

D-3: Locking and logging off of Windows 7

Here's how	Here's why
1 Open Calculator	
2 Click [Start button]	You're going to lock Windows 7 to ensure that your workstation is secure.
3 Click the arrow next to Shut down and choose **Lock**	To lock your workstation. The login screen is shown.
4 Enter your password	Remember, your password is p@ssword.
Press ENTER	To unlock your computer. Your programs are still running.
5 Click **Start** and then click the arrow next to Shut down	To display the options.
Choose **Log Off**	To log off. Windows closes your applications and logs you off.

Unit summary: The Windows 7 environment

Topic A In this topic, you learned how to **log on** to a Windows 7 computer. You identified the **desktop components**. You also learned how to use the mouse.

Topic B In this topic, you used the **Start menu** to open applications. You also used the **taskbar** to switch between open applications, and you identified the components of the taskbar.

Topic C In this topic, you learned how to move a **window** by dragging its title bar. You also learned to resize a window by dragging its edges or corners or by using **Aero Snap**. You used the Control menu buttons to maximize, minimize, restore, and close windows. And you learned how to work with **menus**, **toolbars**, and **dialog boxes**.

Topic D In this topic, you learned how to use **Windows Help and Support**. You used the toolbar to navigate through Help, and you followed links to find information about Windows. You also used the **Search** feature to search for all topics in which a specified word or phrase occurred at least once. Finally, you **locked your computer** and **logged off**.

Review questions

1 What do you call the process of entering a user name and password to gain access to a Windows 7 computer?

2 What's the first thing you see after you log on to a Windows 7 computer?

3 What's the name of the component at the bottom of the desktop?

4 What feature of the taskbar do you use to open applications or access Windows 7 features?

5 What do you call the small pictures on the desktop that you use to open programs?

6 What appears if you hold the mouse pointer over an item on the desktop?

7 How do you switch between applications?

8 What can you do with the buttons in the upper-right corner of any window?

9 What window component has buttons for frequently used commands?

10 Why would you lock your computer?

Independent practice activity

In this activity, you will practice using the Window 7 interface.

1. Log on to a Windows 7 computer. Locate the notification area and display the clock's ToolTip.
2. Open Notepad, Windows Calculator, and WordPad.
3. Lock the workstation.
4. Unlock the workstation. Use the Show Desktop button to display the desktop.
5. Activate the Notepad application.
6. Drag the Notepad window's title bar to the far right of the screen so the window snaps to half the screen size.
7. Make WordPad take up the other half.
8. Drag Notepad down and to the left so it returns to its previous size.
9. Restore WordPad.
10. Minimize WordPad.
11. Maximize WordPad.
12. Close Windows Calendar, WordPad, and Notepad.
13. Use Windows Help and Support to find topics about the Start menu and Aero Peek.
14. Log off the computer.

Unit 2

Files, folders, and libraries

Unit time: 75 minutes

Complete this unit, and you'll know how to:

A Create and manage folders and libraries.

B Create and manage files.

Topic A: Folders and libraries

Explanation

The basic unit of storage on a computer is a *file*. Files can contain documents, programs, configuration settings, pictures, and any other named set of data. The term *content* refers to text files, audio files, video files, e-mail messages, spreadsheets, graphics, and Web files—information that you read or look at or listen to, as opposed to the programs that display that content or run your computer. Managing content on computers can be a challenge because there are so many different types of files.

The use of libraries is new in Windows 7. A *library* is a way to organize files of similar types, regardless of which actual folder the files are stored in. To understand how libraries differ from folders, it helps to first have a general idea of how Windows organizes files.

Every user account on a Windows 7 computer will have personal folders. There is just one set of Public folders, which all users can see and save files in, making sharing files a little easier. A user's personal folders, though, are visible only to that user, though they can be accessed from an administrator account.

Folder hierarchies

The analogy of a filing cabinet is useful for understanding the organization of files on a computer. Each drawer in the cabinet is like a drive on your computer. It can be a hard drive, a DVD drive, a flash card, or any other storage device. The highest level is called the *root* (or root folder or root directory). Files that are not in the root directory are stored in folders, just like papers can be stored inside folders in the file drawer. And just like folders in a filing cabinet, the computer folders can also contain folders. A folder inside another folder is referred to as a *subfolder*.

Note: Folders were originally referred to as "directories" and "subdirectories," and those terms are still used in some environments, but we'll stick with "folder" in this book.

A file or folder's *path* is a complete description of its location. For instance, the actual path to a user's Documents folder is C:\Users*User_Name*\My Documents. In the example shown in Exhibit 2-1, the folder My Documents is in the folder User01, which is in the folder Users, which is on the C: drive. When you have a folder open in Windows Explorer, you can see the complete path in the Address bar at the top of the window, as shown in Exhibit 2-1.

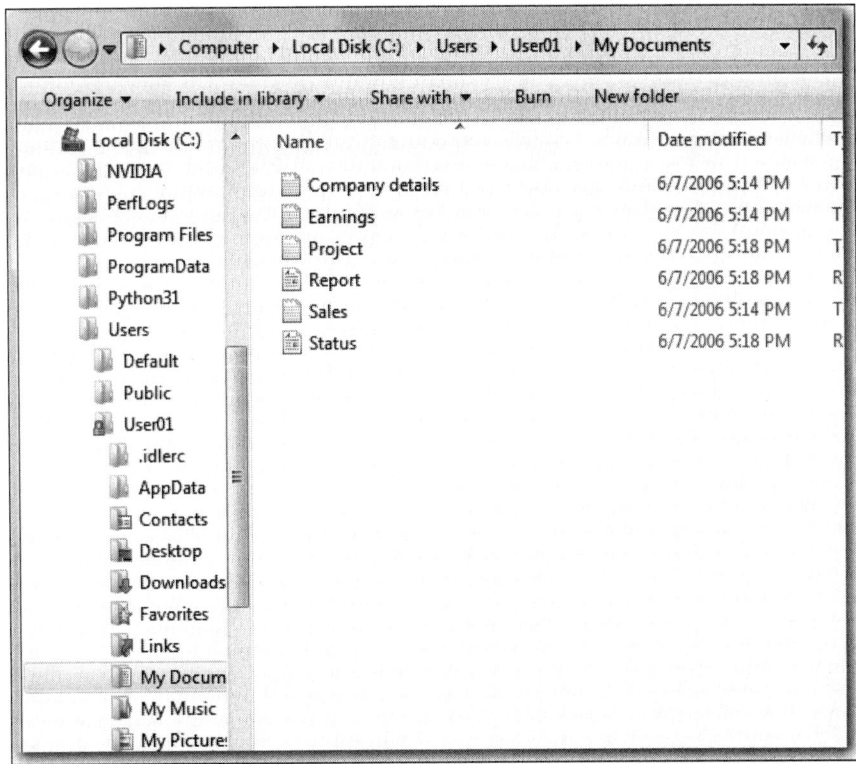

Exhibit 2-1: The folder My Documents is highlighted, and its path is shown in the Address bar

Windows Explorer

As you can see, file and folder paths can quickly get long and complicated. One of the main purposes of Windows Explorer is to hide some of this complication by leaving out the full paths. When you open Windows Explorer, you see various categories like Favorites, recently used files, folders, libraries, and network locations. You can still find actual file locations on your computer, but you might never need to. Exactly what you see in Windows Explorer depends on what location you're looking at and which view options are set.

In Exhibit 2-2, the Pictures library is shown, the files are in List view, and the preview pane is visible. As we'll discuss later, all of these settings can be changed.

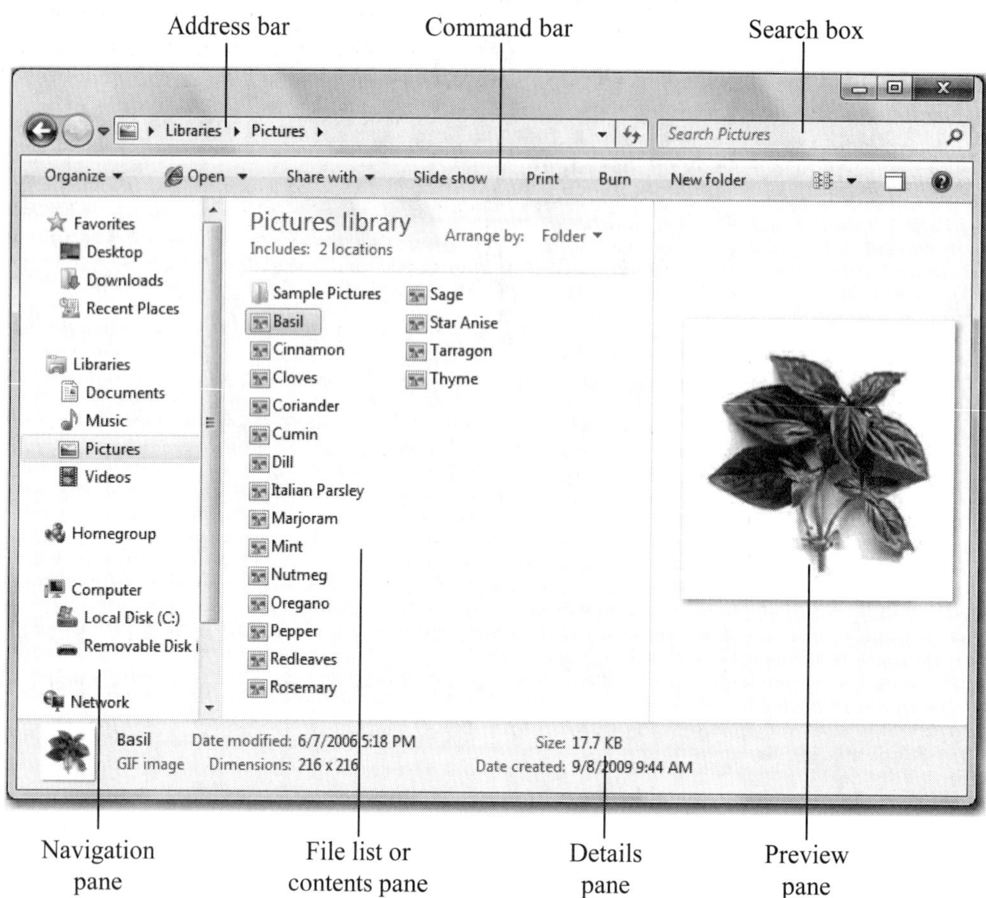

Exhibit 2-2: Windows Explorer with the Pictures library open

There are several ways to open Windows Explorer, and the only difference is the location or library you start in. For instance, if you click Start and choose Computer, Windows Explorer opens at the computer level, with hard disks and other devices shown in the contents pane. If you click the Windows Explorer icon on the taskbar, you'll start with all libraries shown in the contents pane.

The following table describes the components of Windows Explorer.

Component	Description
Address bar	Shows your current location in your computer's folder hierarchy. You can click an arrow next to a folder to see a list of folders beneath it. If you click the Refresh arrow, you will refresh the view to include any recent changes.
Command bar	Contains buttons used to change how the content is displayed, create folders, share files and folders with other users, and restore files to an earlier version. You can also click the Help button to get help with what you're doing. The Command bar is *dynamic*, which means that its buttons change depending on what you're doing in the window at any given time.
Search box	Used to enter words or phrases if you want to search for documents containing those words or phrases. Search terms are often called *keywords*.
Navigation pane	Used to move through the folder hierarchy and other locations, like libraries, removable storage devices, and network locations.
File List pane or contents pane	Displays drives, devices, folders, and files in the location that is selected in the navigation pane.
Details pane	Displays detailed information for the drive, device, folder, or file that is selected in the navigation or contents panes.
Preview pane	Displays the contents of the folder that is selected in the contents pane.

Do it!

A-1: Browsing the folder hierarchy in Windows Explorer

Here's how	Here's why
1 On the taskbar, click the Windows Explorer icon	To open Windows Explorer.
2 In the navigation pane, click **Computer**	You see the hard drives and other storage devices, and their free space and total capacity.
3 Close Windows Explorer	Click the Close button in the upper-right corner of the window.
4 Click **Start**	The upper items in the right pane of the menu (the user name, Documents, Pictures, Music, and Computer) all open Windows Explorer to different locations.
5 Choose **Computer**	Windows Explorer opens to the computer view you saw above, showing the hard dives. It doesn't matter how you open Windows Explorer; the same options are available.
6 In the navigation pane, click **Local Disk (C:)**	Local Disk (C:) Files and folders in the root are shown in the contents pane. Triangles appear to the left of the drive names.
7 In the navigation pane, click the triangle to the left of Local Disk (C:), as shown	Local Disk (C:) To expand the drive in the navigation pane.
8 Expand the Student Data folder	Click the triangle to the left of it in the navigation pane. Note that the folders are not shown in the contents pane yet.
In the navigation pane, click the **Student Data** folder	The folders are shown in the contents pane.
9 In the contents pane, double-click the current unit folder	To open the folder, as selecting it in the navigation pane would do. This folder contains one document, named Introduction.
Observe the Address bar	It shows the current path, which is something like C:\Student Data\Unit_02.

10 In the Address bar, click the down-arrow to the right of Student Data, as shown

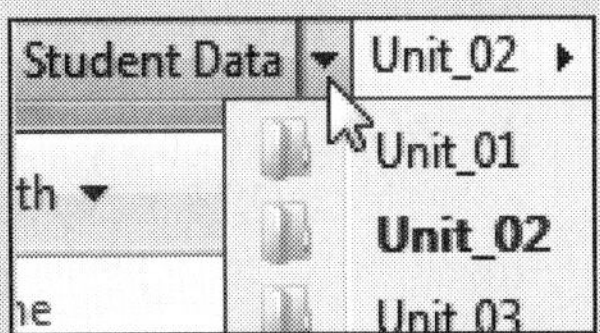

To display a list of folders in that location, with the current folder highlighted.

11 In the Address bar, click **Local Drive (C:)**

To go back up to that level.

12 Navigate to **C:\Users\User01\My Pictures**

In the contents pane, double-click Users, then User01, then My Pictures. Substitute *User01* with your user name, if it's different.

Observe the contents pane

It contains several pictures of spices in Large Thumbnail view.

13 On the Command bar, click the down-arrow next to the View button, as shown

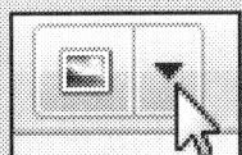

To display a list of View options with a slider. The appearance of the View button changes depending on the current setting.

Drag the slider slowly down to **List**

The thumbnail pictures shrink until, in List view, they are just picture icons.

14 Click [Preview Pane button]

(The Preview Pane button is to the right of the View button.) The preview pane appears.

Select a picture file to see its preview on the right

Close the preview pane

On the Command bar, click the Preview Pane button again.

15 Close Windows Explorer

Libraries

Explanation

A Windows *library* is a collection of related locations that you can see in one contents pane. Your libraries are listed in the navigation pane of Windows Explorer. The built-in libraries include Documents, Music, Pictures, and Videos, and you can add new libraries.

Previous versions of Windows had special-purpose folders for different types of content, and these folders were all subfolders of a personal folder that was automatically created for each user. Some of these folders still exist in Windows 7, but they are now included in the appropriate library.

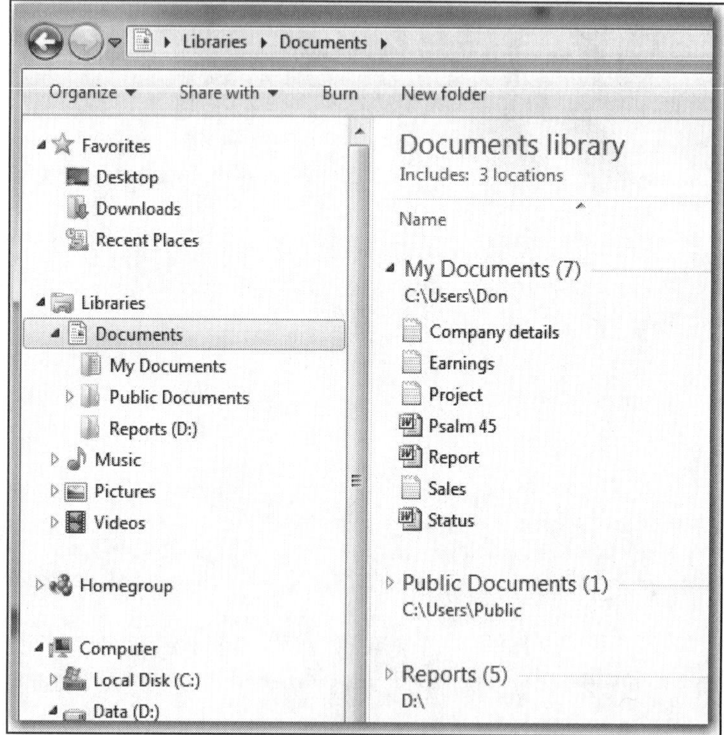

Exhibit 2-3: This Documents library contains three locations

The Documents library, for instance, is not an individual folder, but rather a listing of the files found in the Public Documents folder and in your personal Documents folder. You can add other folders to libraries, too. If, for instance, you store all your Word documents in a folder on an external hard drive, you can add that folder to your Documents library. In the example shown in Exhibit 2-3, the folder D:\Reports has been added to the Documents library.

To see which folders are actually in a given library, select the library in the navigation pane of Windows Explorer. The included locations will be shown in the contents pane, as shown in Exhibit 2-3. Also, you can expand the libraries in the navigation pane and select an individual folder to see only that folder's contents.

Creating and deleting libraries

To create a library, do either of the following:

- In the navigation pane of Windows Explorer, select Libraries; then, on the Command bar, click New library. Enter a name for the library. You can then add locations to your new library.
- Right-click a folder and choose "Include in library," "Create new library." This action automatically creates a library with the name of the selected folder and includes that folder in the library. You can then add more locations.

To delete a library, select it in Windows Explorer and press Delete, or right-click the library and choose Delete. **Note:** Deleting a library does not remove any of the files or folders that were included in the library.

Adding folders to a library

To add a location to a library, follow these steps:

1. In the navigation pane of Windows Explorer, select the library to which you want to add a location.
2. In the contents pane, under the library's title, click the link stating the number of locations (such as "3 locations"). This opens the Library Locations dialog box for that library. See Exhibit 2-4.
3. Click Add. Navigate to and select the desired folder, and click the Include folder button. You are returned to the Library Locations dialog box with the new folder shown.
4. Click OK to return to Windows Explorer.

You can also right-click a folder in Windows Explorer and choose "Include in library," and then select the desired library.

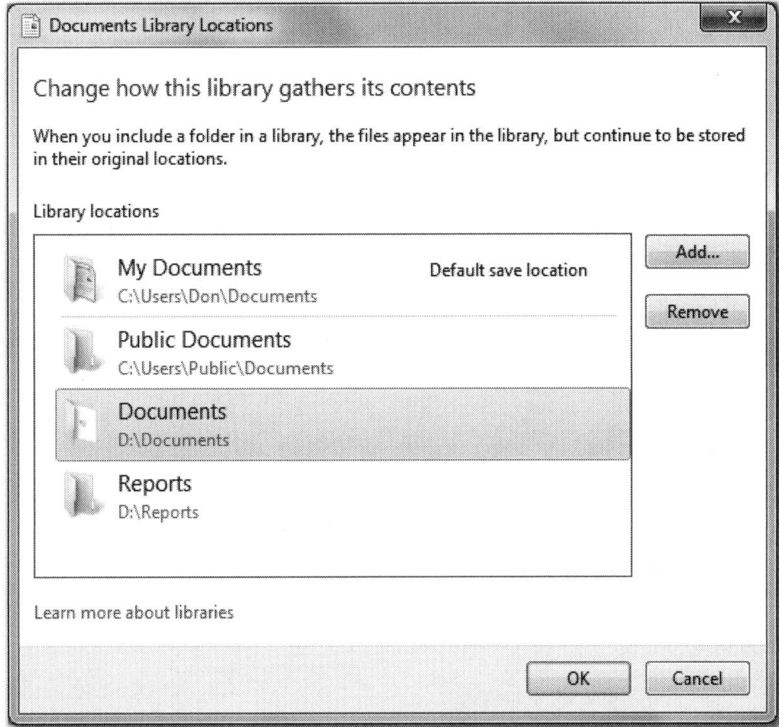

Exhibit 2-4: The Library Locations dialog box for the Documents library

A folder can be included in more than one library. For instance, an online auctioneer might have a library for current items for sale; this library might include a folder for item descriptions and a folder for item pictures. These same folders might also be included in the Documents and Pictures libraries.

If you include one library in another library, all of the folders in the first one will be included in the second, as though you had added them individually. However, the first library name won't appear in the second library.

Removing folders from a library

Reverse the methods above to remove folders from a library:

- in the navigation pane, right-click the folder under the expanded library and choose "Remove location from library."
- With the library displayed in the contents pane, click the number-of-locations link under the library title. Then use the Library Locations dialog box to remove the folder.

Default saving locations and content order

Every library has a default saving location—the actual folder where it will save something that is saved in the library. For instance, if you drag a file to the Documents library, the file will be saved in the My Documents folder by default. You can change the default save location from the Library Locations dialog box. Just right-click a folder and choose "Set as default save location."

You can also use the Library Locations dialog box to change the order in which the locations appear in the library's contents pane. By default, the folders appear in the order in which they were added to the library. To change that order from within the Library Locations dialog box, right-click a folder and choose "Move up" or "Move down."

Do it!

A-2: Using libraries

Here's how	Here's why
1 Open Windows Explorer	Click its icon on the taskbar.
2 In the navigation pane, select the **Documents** library	Several pictures and a folder are shown. The Command bar has a "New library" option. You'll create a library later in this activity.
3 Expand the Pictures library	Pictures My Pictures Public Pictures Click the triangle to the left. The Pictures library currently includes My Pictures and Public Pictures.
4 In the navigation pane, click **My Pictures**	The contents pane shows the files in My Pictures, but not the folder.
Click **Public Pictures**	The Public Pictures folder contains a folder of sample pictures.
5 Click **Pictures**	(In the navigation pane.) To see the contents of both folders again.
6 Under "Pictures library" in the contents pane, click **2 locations**	To open the Library Locations dialog box. Note that My Pictures is the default save location; if you save a file in the Pictures library, the file will be saved in this folder.
7 Click **Add**	You'll add another location to this library.
8 Navigate to the current unit folder	Expand Computer, Local Drive (C:), Student Data, and the current unit folder. It contains the folders Reports and Spice Pics.
9 Select **Spice Pics** and click **Include folder**	You are returned to the Library Locations dialog box, and Spice Pics is now included.
10 In the dialog box, right-click **Spice Pics** and choose **Move up**	It will be moved up in the contents pane.
11 Click **OK**	To return to Windows Explorer.
Observe the contents pane	(You might have to scroll down.) It now shows the pictures from Spice Pics.
12 Navigate to the current unit folder	

13	Right-click the **Reports** folder and choose **Include in library**	In Windows Explorer.
	Observe the shortcut menu	It shows the current libraries and the option to create a new library.
	Choose **Create new library**	A library called Reports is created, and the Reports folder is included in it. You could now add more folders to it.
14	Open the Library Locations dialog box for the Reports library	Select the library in the navigation pane. Then, under "Reports library" in the contents pane, click "1 location."
15	Click **Add**	
	Add **My Documents**	Expand the Documents library, select My Documents, and click Include folder.
16	In the dialog box, right-click **My Documents** and choose **Set as default save location**	
17	Click **OK**	My Documents is now included in the Reports library. A folder can be included in more than one library.
18	In the navigation pane, select the **Reports** library and press DELETE	(You can also right-click Reports and choose Delete.) To remove the library. The folders and files in the library are not deleted.
19	Expand the Pictures library	
	Right-click **Spice Pics** and choose **Remove location from library**	The folder is removed from the library.
20	Close Windows Explorer	

Creating folders

Explanation

To create a folder in the location currently selected in the navigation pane, just click the New folder button on the Command bar. If a library is selected, the new folder will be created as a subfolder of the default save folder for that library. You can also right-click a blank area of the contents pane and choose New, Folder from the shortcut menu.

Folder naming conventions

After you create a folder, you need to name it. A folder name can contain up to 255 characters, including spaces. However, you should try to keep the names short, simple, and meaningful so that they are easy to remember. A folder name can contain any characters except for the following:

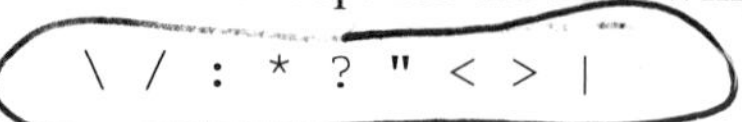

Do it!

A-3: Creating a folder

Here's how	Here's why
1 Open Windows Explorer	
2 Expand the Documents library and select **My Documents**	
3 On the Command bar, click New folder	A new folder appears named "New folder," but the name is selected and editable.
4 Type **Personal**	The name "Personal" will replace "New folder."
Press ENTER	To assign the name to the folder. The new name appears only after you press Enter or click elsewhere on the screen.
5 In the navigation pane, expand the My Documents folder	The folder "Personal" has been added as a subfolder of My Documents and consequently has also been added to the Documents library.
Click **Personal**	The contents pane is empty because this folder doesn't contain any subfolders or files yet.

Renaming folders

Explanation

To rename a folder or library, you need to ensure that it's selected, and then right-click it and choose Rename. You can also select it and press the F2 key. The folder's name is selected to indicate that you can enter a new name. Type the new name and press Enter.

Do it!

A-4: Renaming a folder

Here's how	Here's why
1 In the navigation pane, select **My Documents**	
Press F2	The folder name is highlighted and can be changed.
Press ESC	To cancel the renaming operation.
2 Right-click the **Personal** folder and choose **Rename**	The name is selected and editable.
3 Type **My Stuff** and press ENTER	To rename the folder. The new name replaces the old one.
4 Close Windows Explorer	

Topic B: Working with files

Explanation

Now that you've learned how content is organized on your computer, it's time to learn how to work with your content effectively.

Opening files

To open a file, simply double-click it. The file will open in the program it's associated with. Almost all files you'll encounter are associated with a program, usually the same program that was used to create them. For example, a document file you created in Microsoft Word will automatically open in Microsoft Word. If a file doesn't have an associated program, you'll be asked to choose a program to open it with when you double-click it.

You can recognize file associations by looking at file icons. Files typically have the same icon as the application they were created in, or at least an icon that's similar. Additionally, the file type is described in the preview pane when the file is selected. The file type and the icon tell you and the operating system and other programs what type of file it is. For example, a text file will usually open in Notepad. A Web file will open in Internet Explorer or whatever your default Web browser is.

Do it!

B-1: Opening files in their associated programs

Here's how	Here's why
1 Click **Start** and choose **Documents**	To open Windows Explorer to the Documents library.
2 In the contents pane, select the file named **Report**	This file was provided for you during the classroom setup.
Observe the details pane	At the bottom of the Explorer window.
3 Select the file and observe the details pane	Report — Date modified: 9/9/2009 3:20 PM — Rich Text Document — Size: 11.0 KB The details pane displays file information.
4 Observe the Command bar	The buttons have changed because you selected a document. Remember, the Command bar is dynamic and will change depending on what you're doing and what folder you're in.
5 Double-click **Report**	To open the document in WordPad. This is a Rich Text Format, or RTF, file, and it's associated with WordPad, so it opens automatically in that program.
6 Click [X]	To close WordPad.
7 From the Pictures library, open **Basil**	This GIF file is associated with Internet Explorer.
8 Close Internet Explorer	Click the Close button.

File extensions and associations

Explanation

The operating system determines a file's type by looking at its extension. The file *extension* is a period (or "dot") followed by typically three letters (it can be more or less) after the file name. For example, ".txt" is the extension for text files.

Showing extensions

By default, Windows 7 hides extensions from your view. Many users like to turn on the display of file extensions so that they can more easily identify the types of files they are working with. To make file extensions visible, do this:

1. In Windows Explorer, on the Command bar, click Organize and choose "Folder and search options" to open the Folder Options dialog box.
2. On the View tab, clear the checkbox "Hide extensions for known file types."
3. Click OK.

Changing file associations

To change or set a file type's associated program, right-click the file and choose Open with. Sometimes this shortcut menu offers several programs for you to use immediately, but that won't change the file's association. If you click "Choose default program," though, the Open with dialog box opens, as shown in Exhibit 2-5. Here you can open the file once in a different program, or permanently change the association for all files of that type.

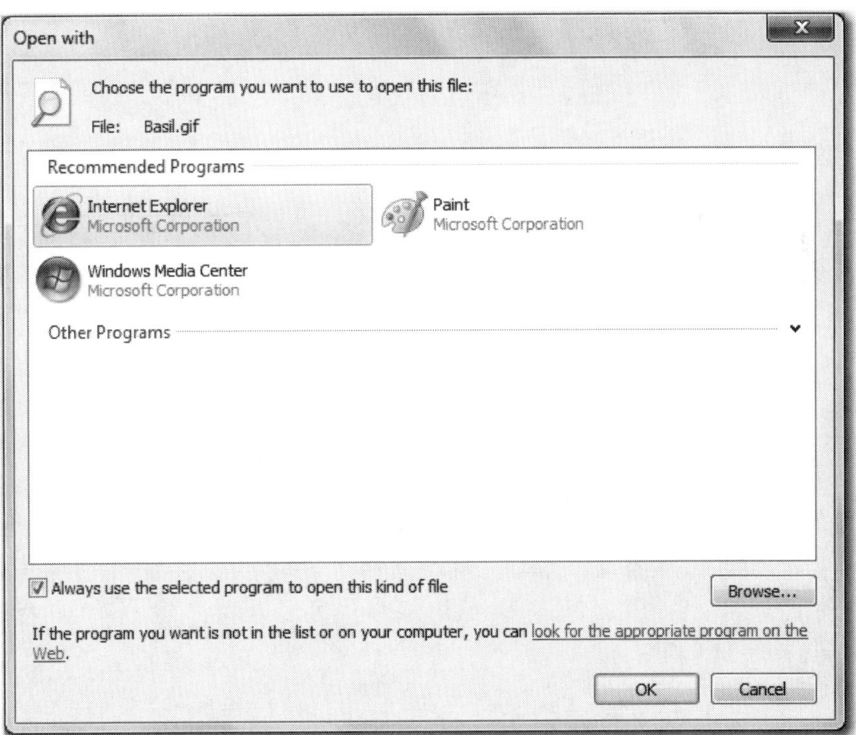

Exhibit 2-5: Use the Open with dialog box to change file associations

Do it!

B-2: Displaying file extensions and changing associations

Here's how	Here's why
1 Select the **Documents** library	The library contains two types of files, as you can see by two types of icons: Notepad and WordPad.
2 On the Command bar, click **Organize** and choose **Folder and search options**	To open the Folder Options dialog box.
3 Activate the View tab	
4 Under Advanced Settings, clear **Hide extensions for known file types**	
5 Click **OK**	
Observe the contents pane	The extensions, .txt and .rtf, are now visible.
6 Select the **Pictures** folder	Some picture files have a .gif extension. These files open in Internet Explorer by default, but you can change this.
7 Double-click **Cinnamon.gif**	It opens in Internet Explorer.
Close Internet Explorer	
8 Right-click **Cinnamon.gif** and choose **Open with**	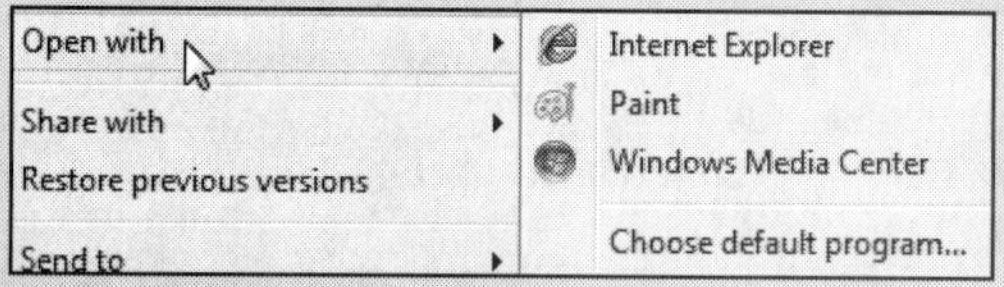 Open with / Share with / Restore previous versions / Send to — Internet Explorer / Paint / Windows Media Center / Choose default program... Note that some file types will have suggested programs for opening a file one time. Doing this will not change the association.
Choose **Choose default program...**	The Open with dialog box opens.
9 Under recommended programs, select **Paint**	
Observe other options in the dialog box	You can browse for a program that's not in the list of recommended programs. There is a checkbox for permanently changing the association.
10 Click **OK**	Cinnamon.gif opens in Paint.
11 Close Paint	
12 Double-click any other .gif file	It opens in Paint instead of Internet Explorer because you changed the file association.
13 Close Paint	

Creating and saving files

Explanation

Files are created in programs (also called *applications*). There are all kinds of programs that can be used to create a wide range of files. For example, you can create files in word processing programs, spreadsheet programs, graphics programs, text editors, music recording programs, and video capture programs.

A *text file* is a very simple file that contains just text. In Windows 7, you can create a text file in Notepad or in Windows 7 itself:

- To create a text file in Notepad, open Notepad and type your text. Then use the Save As dialog box to save the file (preferably in your Documents folder).
- To create a text file by using Windows 7, select the folder in which you want to create the file. Then right-click a blank area in the right pane to open the shortcut menu and choose New, Text Document.

After creating a file (or folder), you need to name it. A file or folder name can contain up to 255 characters, including spaces. Try to keep the names short, simple, and meaningful so that they are easy to remember. Most applications cannot interpret extremely long file names. Like folder names, file names can contain any characters except the following: \ / : * ? “ < > |

The Save As dialog box

The first time you save a document, you’ll need to name it and specify a folder to save it in. To do this, you’ll use the Save As dialog box, shown in Exhibit 2-6. Often, you’ll change a document and then save it with the same name and in the same location. This action is called an *update*, and you need not use the Save As dialog box for it. The Save As dialog box will usually suggest a file extension and show you files of these same type that are already in the selected location. In Windows 7, the Save As dialog box looks like Windows Explorer with a few small differences, as shown in Exhibit 2-6.

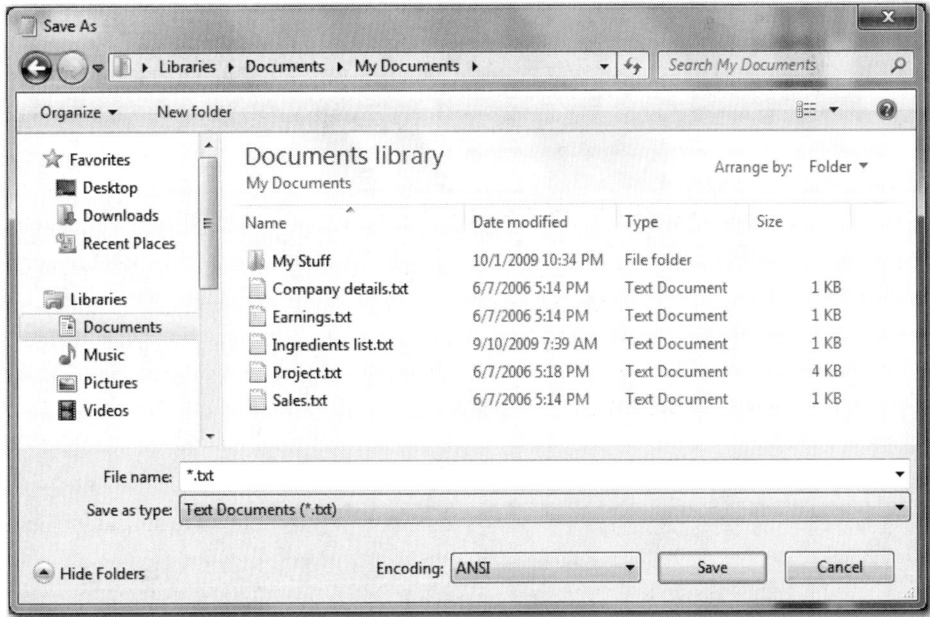

Exhibit 2-6: The Save As dialog box

Do it!

B-3: Creating and saving a text file

Here's how	Here's why
1 Click **Start**	
Choose **All Programs**, **Accessories**, **Notepad**	To create a file with the default name "Untitled."
2 Type your name	
3 Choose **File**, **Save As...**	To open the Save As dialog box.
Observe the Save As dialog box	As shown in Exhibit 2-6. The dialog box appears the first time you save a document. The extension, .txt, is highlighted in the File name box, and you see other text files in the Documents library. You can start typing to assign a file name.
In the File name box, enter **My info**	To specify My info as the name of your file. Don't worry about replacing the ".txt"—Notepad will add it.
4 In the contents pane, double-click **My Stuff**	To open that folder. You just created it so there are no files in it yet.
5 Click **Save**	
Observe the title bar	My info.txt - Notepad The name of the file, "My info," appears.
6 Press ENTER	To move to the next line.
Type your address	
Choose **File**, **Save**	To update the file.

7 Type your telephone number below your address	Press Enter to move to the next line, and then type.
Choose **File**, **Exit**	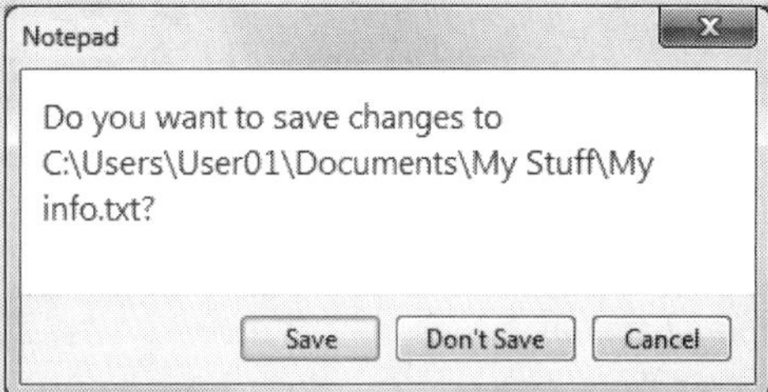 A message box appears, stating that the text in the file has changed and asking if you want to save the changes.
Click **Save**	To save the changes before closing Notepad. If you click Don't Save, the changes made after you last saved the file will be lost. If you click Cancel, the file will not close, and you can continue working in it.

Printing files

Explanation

Most Windows applications provide an option for printing files. For example, to print a WordPad file, you open the file in WordPad and choose File, Print. You can specify several options, such as printing an entire document or a range of pages and selecting the number of copies you want to print.

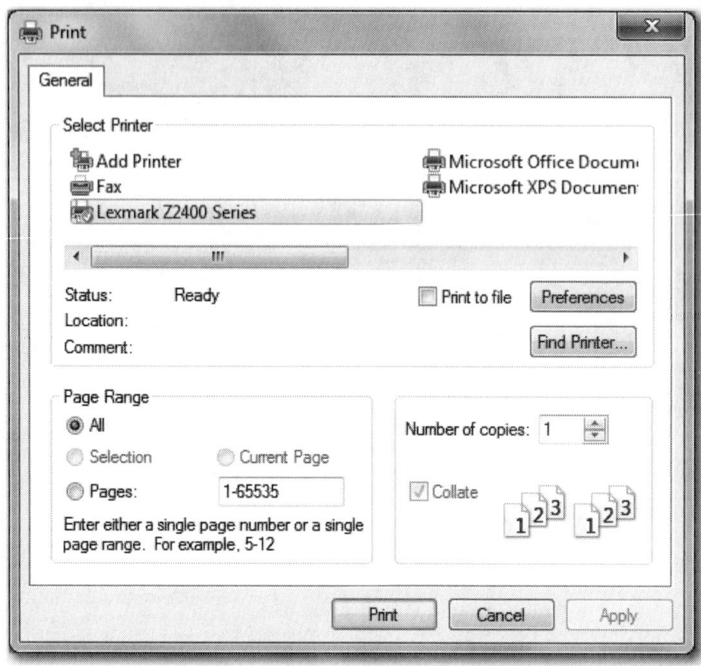

Exhibit 2-7: A sample Print dialog box

Do it!

B-4: Printing a file

Here's how	Here's why
1 Open WordPad	Click Start and choose All Programs, Accessories, WordPad.
2 Type the name and address of one of your friends	Or make up a name and address, if you prefer.
3 Click the File button, as shown, and choose **Save As...**	To open the Save As dialog box. In the Save as type box, Rich Text Format (RTF) is automatically selected as the format for a WordPad file.
In the File name box, enter **My friends**	To specify My friends as the name of your file.
4 Save the file in the Documents library	Click Save. The file should be saved in the My Documents folder by default.
5 Click the File button and choose **Print**	To open the Print dialog box. (A sample dialog box is shown in Exhibit 2-7.) Your Print dialog box might vary depending on the printer installed.
Observe the dialog box	Under Select Printer, the default printer is selected. Under Page Range, All is selected, indicating that all pages in the document will be printed. You can designate specific pages that you want to print. In the list next to Number of copies, 1 appears by default, indicating that one copy is printed unless otherwise specified.
6 Click **Cancel**	To close the Print dialog box without printing.
7 Close WordPad	To close the file and WordPad.

Moving and copying files and folders

Explanation

There are many ways to move and copy files and folders in Windows 7.

Note that when you drag a file or folder, there is a default command associated with that action. For instance, if you drag a file from one folder to the other on the same drive, the default is to move it. If you drag a file between storage devices—say from the hard drive to a flash drive—the default is to copy. To use drag options other than the default, right-click and drag, and choose a command from the shortcut menu.

Moving files and folders

To move a file or folder from one place to another:

- Drag a file or folder from its current location to its new location. As you drag, you'll see a message near the mouse pointer that says "Move to *location*," where *location* is the name of the folder.
- Right-click and drag a file or folder, and then choose Move here from the shortcut menu.
- Select the file or folder you want to move. Click Organize and choose Cut. Open the new location, click Organize, and choose Paste.
- Right-click the file or folder you want to move and choose Cut. Open the new location, right-click a blank area, and choose Paste.
- Select the file or folder you want to move and press Ctrl+X to cut (remove) the selected item. Open the destination folder and press Ctrl+V to paste the item.

Copying files and folders

When you change a copy of a file, the original file is not changed. You might make a copy as a backup, in case the original is changed or lost. You might also make copies to share with co-workers or use copies to try out some changes without losing your original work.

You can copy files and folders from one folder to another and even within the same folder. If you copy a file or subfolder within the same folder, Windows 7 automatically designates the duplicate file as a copy.

There are several ways to copy and paste files and folders:

- Press and hold Ctrl, and drag the file or folder from its current location to its new location.
- Right-click and drag, and then choose Copy here from the shortcut menu.
- Select the file or folder you want to copy. Click Organize and choose Copy. Select the new location, click Organize, and choose Paste.
- Select the file or folder you want to copy. Right-click it and choose Copy. Then right-click the destination folder and choose Paste.
- Select the file or folder you want to copy. Press Ctrl+C to copy the item. Select a destination folder and press Ctrl+V to paste the item into the destination folder.

Opening a folder in a new window

Sometimes you might want to compare the contents of two folders side by side, and it's easier to drag files back and forth between them. Right-click a folder and choose "Open in new window" to open the folder in its own Windows Explorer window.

Do it!

B-5: Moving and copying files

Here's how	Here's why
1 Open Windows Explorer	
In the navigation pane, expand the Documents library and My Documents	My Documents should contain the folder My Stuff, which you created earlier.
Select **My Documents**	To see its contents.
2 In the contents pane, select **My friends**	This is the file you created earlier.
3 Drag My friends toward the My Stuff folder	 (Either in the navigation pane or in the contents pane.) As you drag the file, a transparent icon moves with the mouse pointer.
When the Move to My Stuff message appears, release the mouse button	 When an appropriate destination folder is selected, you will see the message "Move to *folder name*." In this case, you want to move the file to the My Stuff folder.
4 In the navigation pane, select **My Stuff**	This folder now contains two files, My info.txt and My friends.rtf.

Deleting and restoring files

Explanation

When you no longer need a file or folder, you can delete it. Doing so frees up disk space for new content. If you delete the wrong file or change your mind, though, all is not lost. Deleted files are stored in the Recycle Bin, at least for a while.

Deleting files

To delete a file or folder, use any of these methods:

- Select the item and press the Delete key on your keyboard.
- Drag the item to the Recycle Bin.
- Right-click the item and choose Delete.

With all of these methods, Windows will ask you to confirm the deletion.

Restoring files

In Windows, the files and folders you delete are not immediately erased. Instead, they are moved to a special folder called the Recycle Bin. The Recycle Bin gives you a chance to recover items you have deleted.

Items do not remain in the Recycle Bin forever, though. Eventually, they will be permanently deleted from your computer. Windows 7 devotes a limited amount of space to the Recycle Bin. When you delete more items than will fit in that space, Windows permanently deletes the oldest items to fit your most recently deleted items. Also, if you need space to store active files, Windows will permanently delete items in the Recycle Bin and reduce its size to free up room for your active files.

You cannot open items directly in the Recycle Bin. You must restore them first.

To restore an item from the Recycle Bin:

1. Double-click the Recycle Bin to open it.
2. Locate and select the object you want to restore.
3. On the Command bar, click "Restore this item"; or right-click the item and choose Restore. The item will be returned to its original location.

Do it!

B-6: Deleting a file

Here's how	Here's why
1 In the My Stuff folder, select **My info**	You'll delete this file. Files and folders can be deleted in the same way.
2 Press DELETE	
	A message box appears, asking if you want to send the file to the Recycle Bin.
3 Click **Yes**	The My Stuff folder now contains only the My friends file.
4 On the desktop, double-click the **Recycle Bin**	Windows Explorer opens to the Recycle Bin folder. The My info text document appears in the right pane. You'll restore this document.
5 Find and select **My info.txt**	Before anything is selected, the Command bar has a "Restore all items" option; it changes to "Restore this item" when you select something.
6 On the Command bar, click **Restore this item**	The My info document disappears from the right pane and is restored to its original location. You can also restore files to any location by cutting and pasting or by dragging them out of the Recycle Bin.
7 Close the Recycle Bin	
8 Navigate back to the My Stuff folder	The My info text document has been restored to the folder from which it was deleted. The My Stuff folder now contains two files again.
9 Close Windows Explorer	

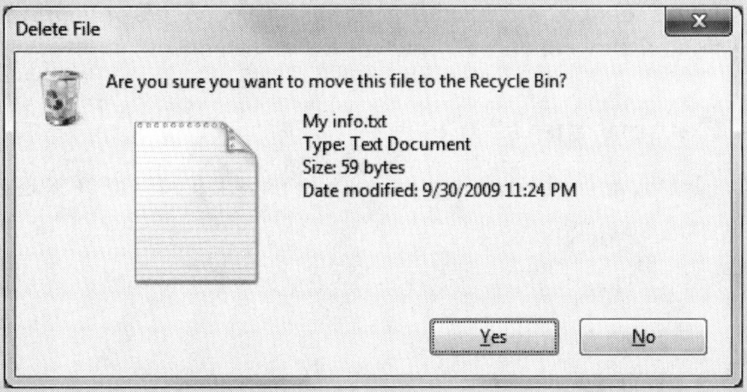

Unit summary: Files, folders, and libraries

Topic A In this topic, you learned that data is stored in files. Each file is stored in a **folder**. Files and folders are organized in a folder hierarchy, with C: as the root folder. You learned that *libraries* are collections of related folders or other locations, and that folders can belong to several libraries. You learned how to navigate in the folder hierarchy, create folders, and rename folders.

Topic B In this topic, you opened files in their **associated applications**. You also created, saved, printed, moved, copied, deleted, and restored files.

Review questions

1 Which of the following are valid names for files? [Choose all that apply.]

A Progress Report

B This/that

C Willy-nilly

D Mine>yours

E L8tr0n

2 When double-clicking a given type of file causes it to open in a corresponding program, we say that this file type is ____________ with that program.

3 Saving a file in Notepad will automatically save it with what extension?

A .doc

B .txt

C .npd

D .text

4 True or false? After you delete a file, you can still get it back by restoring it from the Recycle Bin.

5 True or false? A library can have the same name as one of its folders

6 True or false? Deleting a library deletes its contents.

7 True or false? Deleting a folder deletes its contents.

8 If a library contains more than one folder, how can you tell which folder is the default save location?

9 If you drag a file from your hard drive to a removable flash drive, what is the default action that will occur?

A Moving the file

B Copying the file

C Deleting the file

D Creating a shortcut

10 True or false? You can restore a deleted file only to its original location.

11 True or false? A folder can be included in only one library at a time.

12 If you create a library by right-clicking a folder and choosing “Include in library,” “Create new library,” what will be the default name of the new library?

A New Library

B Library01

C Depends on folder contents

D Same as the folder name

Independent practice activity

In this activity, you will practice navigating your computer’s contents, changing file associations, and copying, moving, and deleting files and folders.

1 Open Windows Explorer. In the navigation pane, select Computer. What is the total capacity and free space of the C: drive? What other drives and devices do you see?

2 Select the Pictures library. On the Command bar, click the down-arrow by the View button and experiment with the slider settings. When you’re done, move the slider to Large icons.

3 Change the file association for .gif files to Internet Explorer. (*Hint:* Use the Open with dialog box.)

4 Hide file extensions for known file types. (*Hint:* Use the Folder Options dialog box.)

5 Navigate to the Documents library and expand its folders. Copy the My Stuff folder to the Public Documents folder, using any method you want. Confirm that the folder is in both locations. Rename the copied folder as **Public Stuff**.

6 Delete the My Stuff and Public Stuff folders from both locations. This will delete the folder contents as well.

7 Open the Recycle Bin and observe the contents. The My Stuff and Public Stuff folders should be in there. Don’t restore them. Close the Recycle Bin.

8 Close all open windows.

Unit 3

Managing content

Unit time: 60 minutes

Complete this unit, and you'll know how to:

A Customize Windows Explorer, and edit file metadata.

B Search the computer for specific content.

Topic A: Working with Windows Explorer

Explanation

There are many ways to customize the way you see files and folders and other information in Windows Explorer. By default, Windows determines a folder's type (music, documents, pictures, etc.) based on what is in the folder, and sets the views and details you see accordingly. You might never need to use anything but the Windows defaults, but the options are there if you want them. There are two main areas where you can change the look and behavior of Windows Explorer and its contents:

- Windows Explorer view options
- The Folder Options dialog box

Windows Explorer settings

You can change the way Windows Explorer displays objects. For example, you can display files as icons or thumbnails; you can display file details; or you can display a simple list of files. You can sort, group, and filter files, and you can show or hide various panes in Windows Explorer.

Changing the view

To change the way objects are shown in the contents pane, either click the View button to switch to the next view option, or click the down-arrow beside the View button and use the slider, shown in Exhibit 3-1.

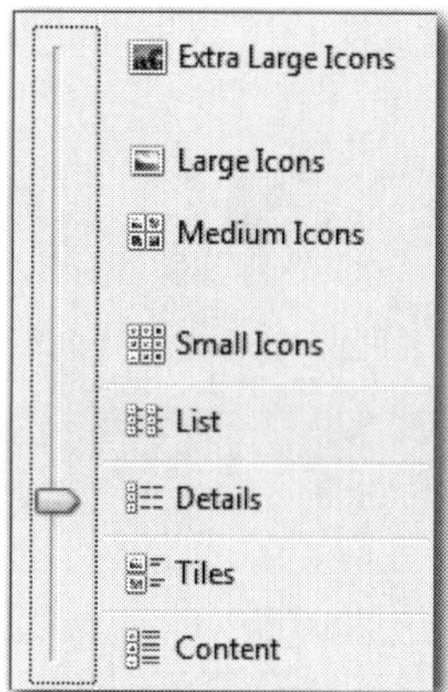

Exhibit 3-1: View options

Changing the layout

To show or hide various panes in Windows Explorer, click Organize and choose Layout; then choose the panes you want to show or hide. You cannot hide the contents pane.

Sorting and arranging files

Windows 7 provides various options for sorting, grouping, and filtering files based on file properties like name, creation date, size, or author. These options enable you to easily work with large sets of files and find just the files you need.

Column headings

The Windows Explorer contents pane shows detail columns that list various file properties, such as the file's name, creation date, author, and so forth. The columns available by default depend on the folder type (e.g., music, documents, or pictures). For instance, a music folder or library shows the file name, artists, album name, number, and song title by default. You can add and remove columns as you wish.

To add or remove columns in the contents pane, right-click any column heading. The shortcut menu shows common headings for that folder type, and you can check or clear headings. You can also choose More to open the Choose Details dialog box, shown in Exhibit 3-2. This dialog box shows you a complete list of available headings.

You can also resize and rearrange columns:

- To resize just two columns, point to the border between the two column headings; when the pointer changes to a double-headed arrow, drag left or right.
- To make columns just wide enough to display their data, right-click a column heading and choose either "Size column to fit" or "Size all columns to fit."
- To change the order of the columns, drag column headings left or right.

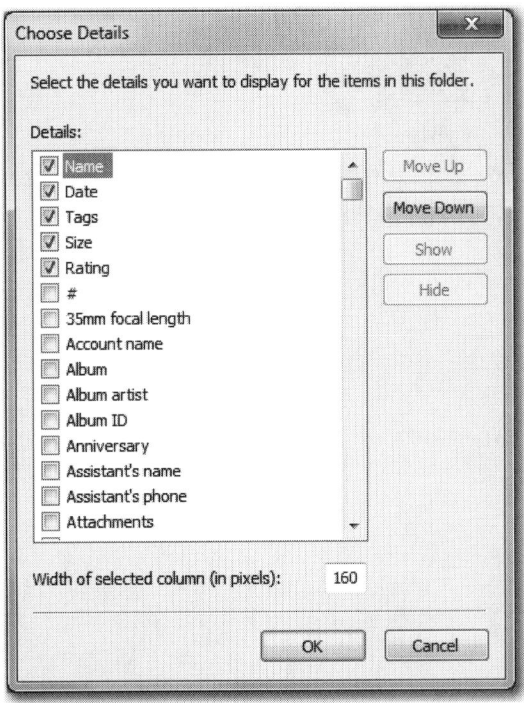

Exhibit 3-2: You can choose which column headings appear in the contents pane

Sorting files

You can sort files and folders by any details shown, in either ascending or descending order, by clicking a column heading. Click the heading once to switch from ascending to descending order; click it again to switch back.

You can also show subsets, such as file names starting with A-H. To select a subset of files, click the down-arrow to the right of a column heading and check the boxes for the desired subsets.

Arranging files

Windows 7 provides a means to arrange, or stack, files with similar attributes. For example, you could create stacks from a selection of music files according to the music genre. Rather than seeing a large list of files or icons, you would see stacks of related files, as shown in Exhibit 3-3. These stacks act like folders in that if you double-click one, you'll see all the files in that stack.

Exhibit 3-3: Stacks of related files

To arrange folders into stacks, click the down-arrow next to the "Arrange by" label in the contents pane.

Do it!

A-1: Customizing Windows Explorer

Here's how	Here's why
1 Open Windows Explorer to the **Pictures** library	
2 Click the down-arrow next to the View button and set the slider to **Details**	 If necessary.
3 Observe the column headings in the contents pane	Default columns for picture folders are Name, Date, Tags, Size, and Rating.
4 Click the **Size** column heading	Files are now sorted from largest to smallest. A small arrow over the heading points down.
Click **Size** again	The order is reversed, going from smallest to largest. The arrow over the heading points up.
5 Click the **Name** heading	The files are in alphabetical order (folders come first).
6 Click the down-arrow to the right of the Name column, as shown	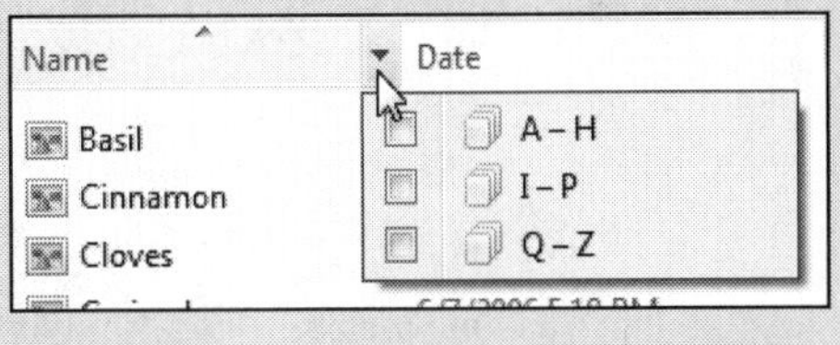 To display possible subsets for this column.
Check **A-H**	To show only the files whose names begin with A-H. The checkboxes remain visible.
Check **Q-Z**	To show this additional subset.
Clear all checkboxes	To see all files again.
7 Press ESC	To close the checkboxes.
8 Right-click any heading	A shortcut menu opens. The checked items are the current detail columns.
Check **Dimensions**	To show the Dimensions column, which shows the picture sizes in pixels.
9 Right-click a column heading and choose **More...**	To open the Choose Details dialog box. The current columns are at the top; the rest are in alphabetical order.
Clear **Tags**	This detail isn't used in these pictures.
10 Click **OK**	The Tags column is hidden.

11 Select the **Music** library and open the **Sample Music** folder	Several sample songs are included with Windows 7.
Observe the column headings	The default headings for music folders are Name, Contributing artists, Album, #, and Title.
12 Next to Arrange by, click the down-arrow and select **Genre**	The songs are arranged into virtual folders, or *stacks*, by genre.
Double-click the **Classical** stack	To see songs in this genre.
Select **Sample Music** again or click the Back button	
13 Click **Genre** and select **Folder**	To remove the stacks organization.
14 Select the **Documents** library	
15 Click **Organize** and choose **Layout**	Menu bar ✓ Details pane Preview pane ✓ Navigation pane ✓ Library pane To display a submenu.
Clear **Navigation pane**	To hide the navigation pane and close the submenu. You'll have to navigate with the Address bar, but you'll have more room in the contents pane.
Show the menu bar	Click Organize, choose Layout, and check Menu bar. This setting shows the old-style Windows Explorer menu bar.
16 Return Windows Explorer to its default appearance	Hide the menu bar and show the navigation pane.
17 Close all open windows	

File details and metadata

Explanation

Some of what you see in the detail columns are general properties of the files. These properties include things like file size, file type, and creation date. These properties are descriptions of the file and usually aren't manually changed. File size, for instance, is a description of how much space the file takes up on the hard disk. You wouldn't change this value manually; it changes when the file is edited and becomes bigger or smaller.

Metadata

Contemporary data files often store *metadata*—data about the data. Metadata provides extra information about a file or folder. For example, when you take a picture with your digital camera, various details about the photo are saved within the picture file, as shown in Exhibit 3-4. Your camera typically records the date, time, exposure settings, and other details that collectively constitute the photo's metadata. Song files can store artist, songwriter, publisher, album art, and digital rights management information.

Exhibit 3-4: Metadata for a picture, with the details pane expanded

Windows 7 enables you to record metadata for any file on your computer. General file properties are recorded automatically, such as the date the file was created, its size, and so forth. Other details you can add, such as the author, rating, and genre. Some details cannot be changed, and you would not normally want to change these. For instance, you wouldn't change data about a camera's settings (e.g., f-stop, focal length) at the time a picture was taken. Also, you can protect a file's metadata from accidental change by making the file read-only.

To add or edit standard metadata for a file:

1. Select a file or folder in the contents pane.
2. If necessary, display the details pane and drag to make it larger. The wider you expand the folder window, the more standard metadata details will be displayed.
3. In the details pane, click a metadata field and enter a new value. With some metadata details, you simply select a value from the available options.

You can also see properties and change metadata by right-clicking a file, choosing Properties, and clicking the Details tab in the Properties dialog box. Sometimes details are shown here that are not shown in the details pane.

Do it!

A-2: Editing metadata

Here's how	Here's why
1 Open the Pictures library	
2 If the details pane is not visible, click **Organize** and choose **Layout**, **Details Pane**	The pane is shown by default but might be hidden from an earlier activity.
Expand the window so it's as wide as your monitor permits	Drag the top edge of the details pane up until you see all of the metadata. Expand the Windows Explorer window if necessary.
3 Click **Garden Gate**	To select the file. Many of the metadata details are filled out.
4 Click one of the spice pictures	These files don't carry much metadata.
5 Click **Rubberband Ball**	This file has metadata fields, but most are not filled out.
6 In the details pane, point to **Add a title** and click	A title can be added or edited.
Enter a title of your choosing	To enter a title for this photo.
Press ENTER	(Or click Save.) To save the information.
7 Right-click **Rubberband Ball** and choose **Properties**	To open the Properties dialog box for the file.
Activate the Details tab	
8 Point to the area to the right of Comments until you see a text box, and then click it	
9 Enter a comment	
Press ENTER	
10 Click **OK**	To close the Properties dialog box.
11 Observe the details pane	The comment you entered is displayed among the other metadata details.
12 Right-click a blank area of the details pane	
Choose **Remove Properties…**	To open the Remove Properties dialog box.

13 Select **Remove the following properties from this file:**	You can also open this dialog box from the Details tab of the file's Properties dialog box by clicking Remove Properties and Personal Information.
14 Check **Title** and **Comments**	
Click **OK**	To close the dialog box.
15 Observe the details pane	The values you entered have been removed, though the fields still exist. You could re-enter the information.
16 Close all open windows	

Topic B: Searching for content

Explanation

There are two places where you will do most of your searching in Windows: the Start menu and Windows Explorer. In general, the Start menu will find only installed programs and files in indexed folders, like those in the libraries. Widows Explorer will search the selected folder or storage device, even if it is not indexed.

Indexing

Windows creates and maintains an index of file names, contents, and metadata for faster searching. When you search for keywords, Windows searches the index rather than actual files, making the search faster in most cases.

By default, Windows indexes folders included in libraries and other frequently used folders. Program and system folders are not usually indexed. These are large and rarely searched folders, and indexing them would slow down average search times.

Managing indexed locations

As with many Windows 7 options, you might never need to manually change indexing settings, but it's good to know what's happening when you search for something. If you've already looked at the advanced attributes of files or folders, you've seen a checkbox that allows the contents to be indexed. Allowing indexing, though, is not the same as ensuring indexing. That checkbox is there so you can prevent a folder from being indexed.

The simplest way to ensure that a folder is indexed is to include it in a library, because all library folders get indexed automatically. Also, when you search a folder that's not indexed, Windows offers you the option of adding it to the index. Be careful not to do this for folders you don't search regularly.

To see or change which folders are indexed:

1. Click Start, type "index" in the search box, and click Indexing Options to open the Indexing Options dialog box.
2. Click Modify to open the Indexed Locations dialog box, shown in Exhibit 3-5. Here, you can add or remove locations.

You might rarely need to use the Indexed Locations dialog box, but if you accidentally tell Windows to add a large folder or drive to the index, you'll want to remove it so it doesn't slow down your everyday operations.

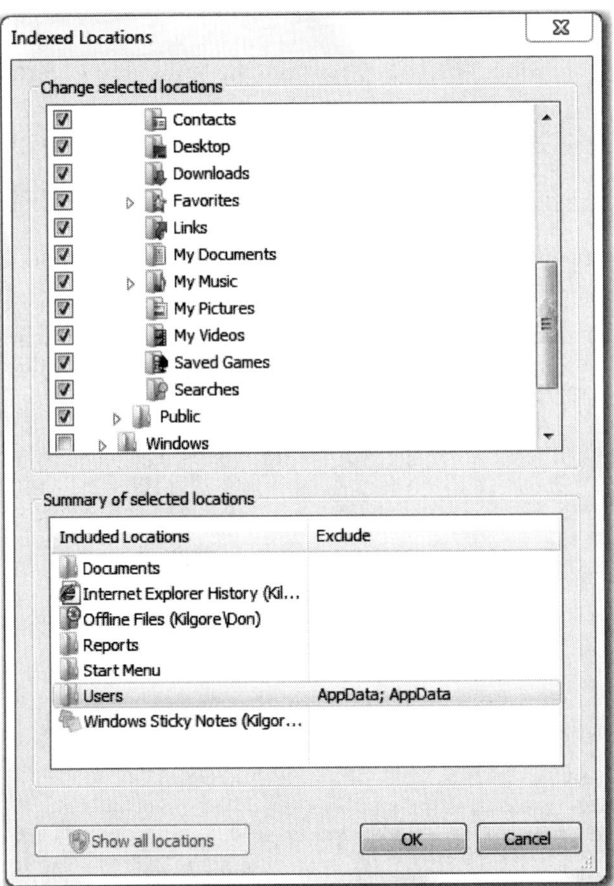

Exhibit 3-5: The Indexed Locations dialog box

Folder search options

Other important search settings are found on the Search tab of the Folder Options dialog box, shown in Exhibit 3-6. They determine how Windows searches folders in three categories:

- **What to search** — By default, Windows searches for file names only. If you want to find words or phrases within documents that are in non-indexed locations, you'll need to change this setting.
- **How to search** — Specify whether to search subfolders and to return partial matches.
- **When searching non-indexed locations** — Specify whether to include system folders and compressed files when searching non-indexed locations.

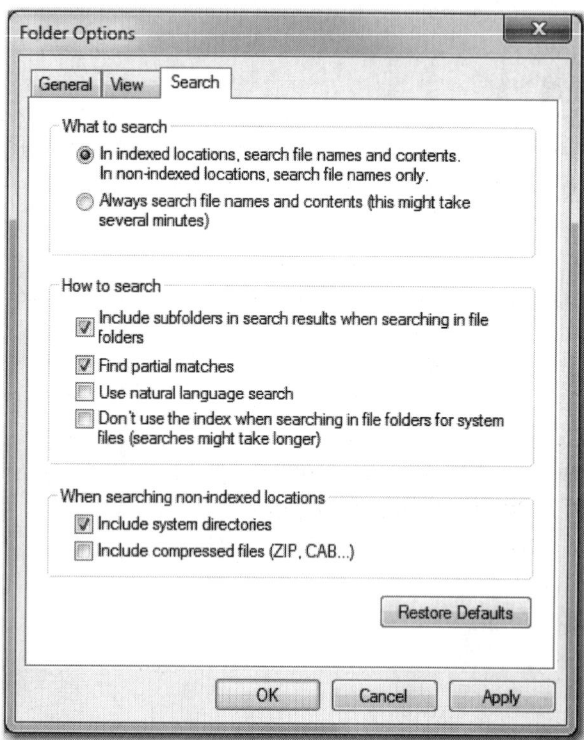

Exhibit 3-6: The Search tab of the Folder options

Searching from the Start menu

At the bottom of the Start menu is a search box. When you open the Start menu, the insertion point is already in this box, so you don't have to click it—just start typing. You can search for documents from here, and you can run programs. For instance, if you type "calc" and press Enter, the Calculator program will open. This search box, in part, takes the place of the Run command found in earlier versions of Windows.

A Start-menu search will find installed programs, indexed files, and recently opened files only. So, use it for things like finding that cover letter you wrote last week. If you're looking for an obscure configuration file buried in a program folder, or looking for a document on a flash drive, you'll need to search in Windows Explorer.

Searching in Windows Explorer

In the upper-right corner of Windows Explorer is a search box that you can use to search whatever folder or device is selected in the navigation pane and shown in the contents pane. By default, subfolders are also searched.

This search looks at file names, file properties and metadata, and file contents, when applicable. All of these details can be searched whether or not the folders are indexed, depending on the search settings discussed previously. If the folders are not indexed, the search might take longer, and a prompt at the top of the contents pane will ask if you want to add the folder to the index.

Some search suggestions

Here are a few tips for refining your searches:

- **Use wildcards** — Wildcards are symbols that take the place of other letters. An asterisk (*) represents zero or more letters. By default, the search will return partial matches, but only at the beginning of a word, not in the middle or end. For instance, searching on **proj** will return "Project" and "projected"; searching on ***ject** will return these, as well as "reject" and "rejected"; searching on **ject** will not return any of these.
- **Use quotation marks** — Sometimes you can find a document by remembering a phrase in it. If you start your search terms with a quotation mark ("), only examples of those words in that order will be returned. So, entering **high school** will return any documents with both words, whether or not they are together, while searching on **"high school** will return only results with that exact phrase.
- **Filter the search** — You can refine a search by specifying things like date modified, file size, and file type. The filters available change depending on which files are in the unfiltered results.

Note that searches are not case sensitive, even if quotation marks are used.

Saving searches

If you often perform the same search on the same location, you can save that search for future reference. Recent search terms are saved in the search box, but a saved search keeps both the terms and the location. To save a search after you've performed it, click "Save search" on the Command bar and enter a name. The saved search will appear in the navigation pane under Favorites.

Do it!

B-1: Searching for file names and contents

Here's how	Here's why
1 Click **Start**	The insertion point is already in the search box at the bottom of the menu
2 Enter **overview**	Two files are found: Project and Report. These come up because they contain the word "overview" and they are in the Documents library, which is an indexed location.
3 Press ESC twice	To close the Start menu.
4 Open Windows Explorer	
5 In the navigation pane, select the current unit folder	There are several subfolders.
6 In the search box, enter **overview**	A bar at the top of the contents pane tells you that the location isn't indexed and asks if you want to index it. Close this bar (click the X at the right end of it).
Observe the results	The file Overview is returned because it's in "Find," a subfolder of the current unit folder. By default, when you search a folder, its subfolders are searched also.
7 In the search box, enter **sa**	Windows begins looking as you type, and the files Sales and Sage are found.
Continue typing so the search term is **sausage**	No files are returned because "sausage" does not appear in any file names. If the word is in a file's *contents*, you wouldn't know, because by default, contents are not searched in non-indexed locations.
8 In the navigation pane, select the current unit folder again	To close the search and return to the folder contents.
9 Click **Organize** and choose **File and search options**	To open the Folder Options dialog box.
Activate the Search tab	
10 Under What to search, select **Always search file names and contents**	So that Windows will search file contents even when you search non-indexed locations. Note the other options on this tab of the dialog box.
Click **OK**	To close the dialog box.
11 Click in the search box and select **sausage**	Recent search terms are saved in the search box. Files appear that contain the word "sausage."

12 On the Command bar, click **Save Search**	The default name is "sausage." You'll keep this.
Click **Save**	The saved search appears under Favorites. You can run this search any time by clicking it.
13 In the navigation pane, select **Libraries**	
14 In the search box, enter **corbis**	All libraries are indexed by default.
Observe the results	Several pictures are returned.
15 Select one of the returned pictures and observe the details pane	Expand it if necessary. These photos are provided by Corbis, an image company. The search also looks at metadata in indexed locations or when the "always search contents" option is used.
16 Close Windows Explorer	

Unit summary: Managing content

Topic A

In this topic, you learned how to change the way Windows Explorer arranges and displays files and other objects. You also learned how to edit a file's **metadata** in the details pane.

Topic B

In this topic, you learned how to search for content on your computer. You learned why Windows **indexes** some folders to speed up searches. You also learned about the difference between a Start-menu search and a Windows Explorer search, and you learned how to search file contents in non-indexed locations. Finally, you learned how to save searches.

Review questions

1 True or false? New folders you create are set to the General Items type until you manually change them.

2 What does clicking a column heading in Windows Explorer's contents pane do?

A Sorts the files on that column

B Expands and collapses the column

C Opens the Column Heading dialog box

D Makes a clicking sound

3 True or false? Different folder types show different detail columns.

4 The details pane shows more data about the selected file. What is another name for this data about the data?

A Datadata

B Metadata

C Interdata

D Duodata

5 True or false? The details shown in the details pane are stored in Windows Explorer and are not copied when you copy the file to another system.

6 True or false? If you want to use a certain picture on a folder icon, the picture has to be in that folder.

7 True or false? If you add a folder to the Documents library, the folder will be indexed automatically.

8 True or false? If you want to search the internal contents of files in a folder, you need to index the folder first.

9 Entering **oin** in the search box would return which of the following? [Choose all that apply]

A coin

B oink

C tenderloin

D appointment

E ointment

10 If you want to search for a specific phrase, you should enter search terms starting with what symbol?

A *

B =

C >

D “

Independent practice activity

In this activity, you will change the way Windows Explorer displays files and information about files.

1 In Windows Explorer, select the Pictures library.

2 If necessary, set the View slider to Details.

3 Remove the Rating column. Add the Type column. Right-click the heading and choose “Size all columns to fit.”

4 Rearrange the columns as follows: Name, Type, Dimensions, Size, Date. (*Hint:* Drag column headings left or right to rearrange columns.)

5 From the Arrange by list, select Month.

6 Select the picture Rubberband Ball. Expand the details pane, if necessary.

7 In the metadata, enter your name as the author, and click Save.

8 Close all open windows.

9 Click Start. Type your name in the search box. Click the picture name in the menu.

10 Close the picture.

Unit 4

Customizing the environment

Unit time: 75 minutes

Complete this unit, and you'll know how to:

A Customize your desktop and Start menu.

B Use Windows 7 gadgets.

C Configure system settings by using the Control Panel.

Topic A: Icons and shortcuts

Explanation

In general, an *icon* is a little picture that represents a program, file, hard disk, or other object on your computer. As you'll see, taskbar icons behave differently than icons on the desktop. A *shortcut* provides a link to an object that is somewhere else on your computer and is represented by an icon. On the desktop, a shortcut's icon has a little curved arrow in the lower-left corner of it. Double-clicking a desktop shortcut is equivalent to navigating to the corresponding object's location on the computer and double-clicking the object.

Taskbar icons

By default, Windows 7 has three icons pinned to the taskbar: Internet Explorer, Windows Explorer, and Windows Media Player. You can remove these or add to them as you wish.

When you open a program by clicking a pinned taskbar icon, the icon appears highlighted, but Windows does not add another icon to the taskbar. This differs a little from previous versions of Windows, in which starting a program from a Quick Launch icon would still add a separate button to the taskbar. If you open a program through the Start menu or some other way, an icon will appear on the taskbar, and it will be indistinguishable from the icons already pinned there. You can drag icons on the taskbar to change their order.

Jump lists

If you right-click a taskbar icon, you'll see a shortcut menu like the one shown in Exhibit 4-1. This menu, called a *jump list*, usually shows recent or frequently opened documents or locations related to that program. For instance, the shortcut menu for Internet Explorer lists recently opened Web sites, allowing you to open those sites directly. Another way to open a jump list is to drag upward on the taskbar icon—this won't move the icon; it'll just open the shortcut menu.

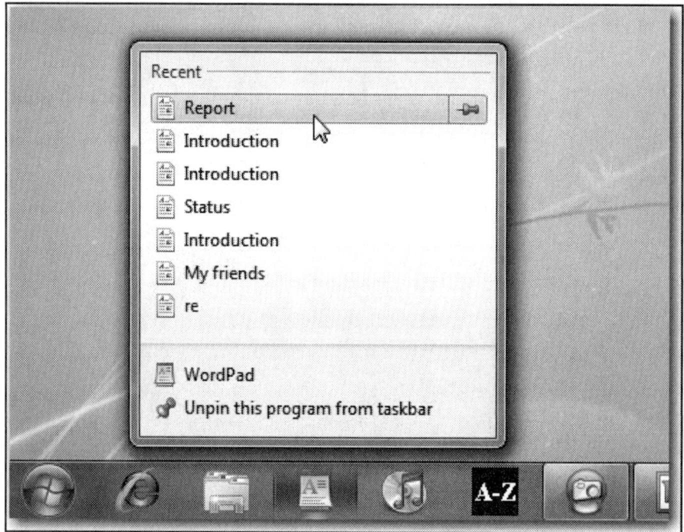

Exhibit 4-1: A jump list for WordPad, showing recent documents

Start menu shortcuts

All programs installed on your computer can be run from the Start menu in one way or another. By default, the left side of the Start menu contains a few programs. As you use Windows over time, that part of the Start menu will change to reflect recently and frequently used programs. If you want a program to stay on the Start menu regardless of how often you use it, you can pin it there. To do so, right-click the program name and choose Pin to Start Menu. That program will now stay in the top section of the Start menu's left pane, over a faint dividing line. As with the taskbar icons, you can rearrange these pinned icons by dragging them.

Some Start menu shortcuts have arrows to the right of them. If you click one of these arrows, or just point to a shortcut, Windows will display a list of documents recently opened in that program. This list is like the jump list that appears when you right-click a program's button on the taskbar.

Do it!

A-1: Adding shortcuts to the Start menu and taskbar

Here's how	Here's why
1 Click **Start** and observe the recently used programs	(On the left side of the Start menu.) There are some default programs there, plus any that you have used during this course.
2 Choose **All Programs**, **Accessories**	You'll pin a program to the Start menu.
3 Right-click **Notepad** and choose **Pin to Start Menu**	To pin the Notepad program to the Start menu.
4 Click **Back**	(At the bottom of the menu.) To return to the main Start menu. Notepad is at the top of the menu, over a light dividing line. It will stay there now, regardless of how much you use the program.
5 In the Start menu, click the arrow to the right of Notepad	To display any recent text documents. Clicking one of these will open it in Notepad.
6 Pin WordPad and Calculator to the Start menu	Right-click each program (in All Programs, Accessories) and choose Pin to Start Menu.
7 In the Start menu, drag Calculator to the top of the list of pinned programs	You can rearrange these as you see fit.
8 In the Start menu, right-click **WordPad** and choose **Pin to Taskbar**	A new icon appears on the taskbar.
9 On the taskbar, right-click the **WordPad** button	(Or drag upward on it.) A shortcut menu—called a jump list—opens, showing recent documents and related commands.
Click a blank area of the desktop	To close the shortcut menu.

Desktop shortcuts

You can create program, folder, and document shortcuts on your desktop. (You have to double-click these icons to start the target programs.) For instance, if you often look at a contact list created in Microsoft Excel and stored in your Documents library, you can create a desktop shortcut to that spreadsheet file. Then if you double-click that shortcut, the spreadsheet will open in Excel.

Keep in mind that the desktop is folder, just like your Documents folders. The Desktop folder is unique in that you see all of its files on the desktop. You can also see its files by navigating in Windows Explorer to your user's desktop folder, which would be something like C:\Users\User01\Desktop. Long path names like that are why it's handy that desktop shortcuts have a little arrow on them—the arrow indicates whether an icon is a shortcut or if the file is really stored on the desktop (that is, in the Desktop folder).

You can also create shortcuts to hardware devices, such as disk drives and printers. You can place shortcuts in folders as well as on the desktop and Start menu. In any case, when you need to work with the original item, you simply double-click the shortcut.

Creating shortcuts on the desktop

Windows 7 provides a couple of ways to create shortcuts:

- Right-click the object to open the shortcut menu and choose Send To, Desktop (create shortcut).
- Point to the object you want to create a shortcut for. Click with and hold down the right mouse button, and drag the object to the desired destination. Release the mouse button to open the shortcut menu, and then choose Create Shortcuts Here.

Arranging desktop icons

Some people like to keep their desktop tidy and free of documents and shortcuts, while others prefer to store all their frequently used documents right in plain view. If you are in the latter group, you might find that your entire desktop is eventually covered with icons.

There are a few ways to arrange your desktop icons to make them easier to sort through. Of course, the first step is to delete the icons you never use. After that, to arrange and configure desktop icons, right-click a blank area of the desktop and choose one of the following from the shortcut menu:

- **View** — Choose the size of the icons, whether to allow Windows 7 to arrange them automatically, whether they should be kept lined up automatically, or whether to show any at all.
- **Sort By** — Choose whether to arrange icons by name, size, type, or the date they were modified.

As with items in folders, larger desktop icons might show you a preview of the documents or pictures.

Do it!

A-2: Adding shortcuts to the desktop

Here's how	Here's why
1 Click **Start** and choose **All Programs**, **Accessories**	You'll create a desktop shortcut for the Paint program.
2 Right-click **Paint** and choose **Send To**, **Desktop (create shortcut)**	To create a shortcut on the desktop.
Observe the Paint shortcut icon	You can rename it if you want to; you rename shortcuts the same way you rename any file or folder.
3 In Windows Explorer, navigate to the **Sample Pictures** folder in the Pictures library	
4 Right-click and drag any picture onto the desktop	
Release the mouse button and choose **Create shortcuts here**	The picture file's icon appears with a little arrow in the corner, indicating that it's a shortcut. The icon is still a thumbnail of the picture.
5 Double-click the picture shortcut	The picture opens in Photo Viewer.
6 Close Photo Viewer	
7 Right-click the desktop and choose **View**	
Observe the View menu	You can choose the size of your icons, whether they're arranged automatically and kept lined up, or whether they're shown at all.
8 Choose **Large Icons**	To increase the icon size.
9 Right-click the desktop and choose **View**, **Auto Arrange icons**	To arrange the icons automatically. This is a toggle menu choice, meaning that you choose it again to disable it.
10 Right-click the desktop and choose **Sort By**, **Name**	To arrange the icons by name.
11 Sort the icons by size	
12 Sort the icons by name again	

Further customizing the Start menu and taskbar

Explanation

Aside from adding and removing icons, you can customize the taskbar and Start menu in other ways. If the taskbar is not locked, you can drag it to any edge of the screen, and you can use smaller icons so it takes up less space.

You can customize the Start menu in many ways, as shown in Exhibit 4-2. For instance, you can change the number of programs shown on the list of recent programs, or you can set Windows so it does not store or show a list of recently opened items.

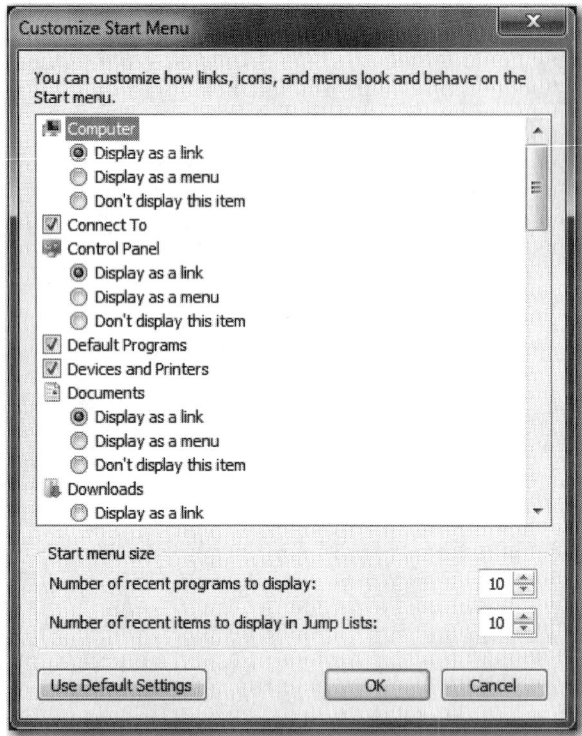

Exhibit 4-2: Options for customizing the Start menu

Do it!

A-3: Customizing the Start menu and taskbar

Here's how	Here's why
1 Right-click a blank area of the taskbar and choose **Properties**	To open the Properties dialog box for both the taskbar and the Start menu.
2 Check **Use small icons**	
Click **Apply**	To apply the change without closing the Properties dialog box. Smaller icons are now used, and the taskbar is smaller as a result.
3 Activate the Start Menu tab	
Observe the options under Privacy	You can set Windows so it does not store or show recently opened items.

4 Next to "Power button action," click the down-arrow, as shown	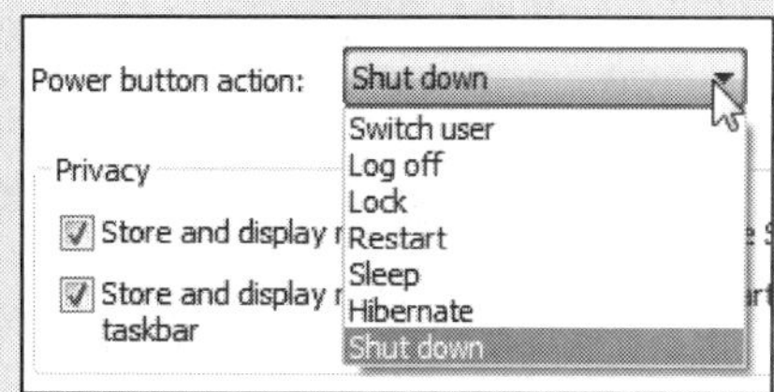 To display a list of actions you can set for the power button. (It's the button at the bottom of the right pane in the Start menu.) It says Shut down by default, but you can change that.
Select **Lock**	
5 Click **Customize**	To open the Customize Start Menu dialog box.
Observe the list of Start menu options	Scroll down to see them all. Under this list you can also change the number of recent programs and documents displayed.
6 Under "Start menu size," change "Number of recent programs to display" to **15**	Use the up arrow, or just select the number and enter 15.
7 Click **OK**	To close the Customize Start Menu dialog box and return to the Properties dialog box.
8 Click **Apply**	To apply the changes without closing the Properties dialog box.
9 Click **Start** and observe the menu	(Leave the Properties dialog box open.) There is more room for items on the menu's left side. This area will fill out as you use the computer. The Power button now says Lock.
Click **Start**	To close the menu and return to the taskbar properties.
10 On the Start Menu tab, click **Customize** and return the Start menu size to **10**	
Click **OK**	
11 Change the power button action back to **Shut down**	Use the Power button action list on the Start Menu tab in the Properties dialog box.
12 Activate the Taskbar tab	
13 Clear **Use small icons**	
Click **OK**	To apply the changes and close the Properties dialog box.

Removing icons and shortcuts

Explanation

Removing a shortcut or a taskbar icon won't affect the actual application, file, or folder that it refers to; it just deletes the shortcut.

Removing taskbar icon and Start menu shortcuts

You can remove both pinned and automatically added icons from the Start menu and taskbar. You might remove pinned items if you no longer use them regularly. Generally, you won't need to remove the items that have been automatically added because as you use new programs, old items will be removed for you.

To remove a taskbar icon:

1 Right-click the icon on the taskbar.
2 Choose "Unpin this program from taskbar."

To remove a pinned menu item:

1 Open the Start menu.
2 Right-click the item and choose Unpin from Start Menu.

To remove an item from the Start menu (from below the separator line):

1 Open the Start menu.
2 Right-click the item and choose "Remove from this list."

Removing desktop shortcuts

Windows 7 provides several ways to delete desktop shortcuts. All of these methods place the shortcut in the Recycle Bin. If you delete a shortcut by mistake, you can restore it from the Recycle Bin.

Here are three ways to delete a shortcut:

- Right-click the shortcut and choose Delete.
- Drag the shortcut icon to the Recycle Bin.
- Select the shortcut and press Delete.

With all three methods, Windows will ask you to confirm the deletion, as shown in Exhibit 4-3.

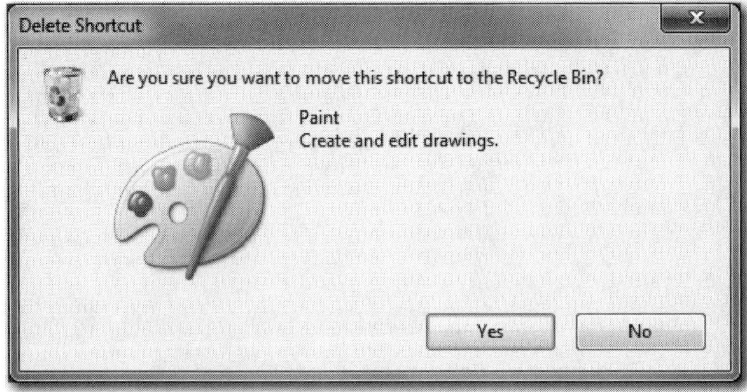

Exhibit 4-3: Confirmation for deleting a shortcut

Do it!

A-4: Removing Start menu shortcuts and taskbar icons

Here's how	Here's why
1 Click **Start**	You're going to delete one shortcut from the Start menu and unpin another.
2 Right-click **Calculator** and choose **Unpin from Start Menu**	To unpin the shortcut from the Start menu.
3 On the desktop, right-click the **Paint** shortcut icon and choose **Delete**	The message box prompts you to confirm the deletion to avoid accidentally deleting the shortcut.
4 Click **Yes**	The shortcut is deleted from the desktop.
5 Delete the desktop shortcut to the sample picture	Use any method you want.
6 On the taskbar, right-click the WordPad icon and choose **Unpin this program from taskbar**	The WordPad icon is removed without confirmation.

Adding a folder to Favorites

Explanation

Although the Favorites list is populated with some shortcuts by default, you can add any folder you wish. Adding a folder to the Favorites list ensures that it's easily accessible no matter which folder you're currently working in.

To add a folder to Favorites, just drag it to the list. A separator line will help you figure out where to drop it, depending on where you want it in the list. This is just a shortcut, so if you delete the shortcut, you won't delete the original. To remove the folder from Favorites, right-click it and choose Delete.

Do it!

A-5: Adding a folder to the Favorites list

Here's how	Here's why
1 In Windows Explorer, navigate to the Student Data folder	But don't open the current unit folder.
2 Drag the current unit folder from the contents pane to the Favorites list	You can drop the folder in the list or right on the word Favorites. A separator line will appear to help you see where you're going to drop the folder.
3 Under Favorites, select the current unit folder	To verify that the folder opens in the contents pane.
4 Under Favorites, right-click the current unit folder and choose **Remove**	(Don't use the one in the contents pane!) To remove the link from your Favorites list. This action removes only the shortcut, not the folder.
5 Close Windows Explorer	

Topic B: Gadgets

Explanation

Gadgets are small programs whose interfaces sit on your desktop, as shown in Exhibit 4-4. They usually perform a single, simple function that you might use often but don't need to give your full attention to. Examples include a clock, a calculator, sticky notes, news feeds, and small games and slide shows. In Windows Vista, gadgets were loaded into the Windows Sidebar, but they could be put right on the desktop. The Sidebar was an unnecessary use of screen space and has been discontinued in Windows 7. (Actually, the sidebar program still runs for gadgets, but there's no sidebar on the desktop.)

Exhibit 4-4: Gadgets on the desktop

Adding and moving gadgets

You add new gadgets from the Gadget Gallery, shown in Exhibit 4-5. To open the Gadget Gallery, right-click a blank area of the desktop and choose Gadgets. Once you're in the gallery, you can right-click the gadget of your choice and choose Add, or just double-click the gadget to add it.

The gallery starts out with just a few gadgets, but the "Get more gadgets online" link gives you access to thousands of gadgets with all kinds of functions.

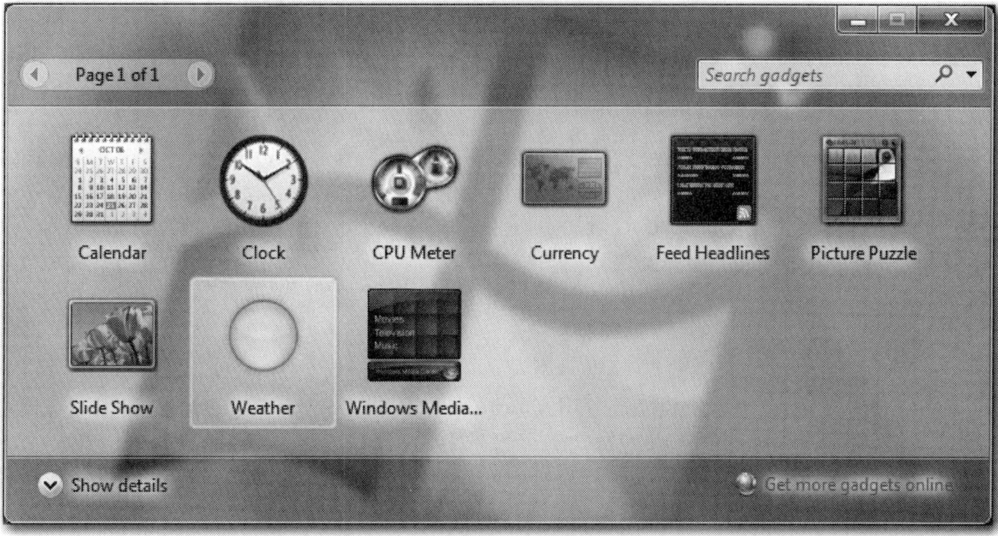

Exhibit 4-5: The Gadget Gallery

Gadget options

Many gadgets have properties you can set. For instance, you can choose different colors for the sticky notes or set the clock to stay on top of open windows. When you point to a gadget, its control buttons appear to the right of it. Some gadgets will have a settings button that looks like a wrench, and this button will open the gadget's settings. Depending on the gadget, you might see some different control buttons. The clock gadget's settings are shown in Exhibit 4-6.

You can right-click a gadget to display a shortcut menu that contains different commands depending on the gadget. Some gadgets have no settable options, and some have a resize button that will make the gadget temporarily larger.

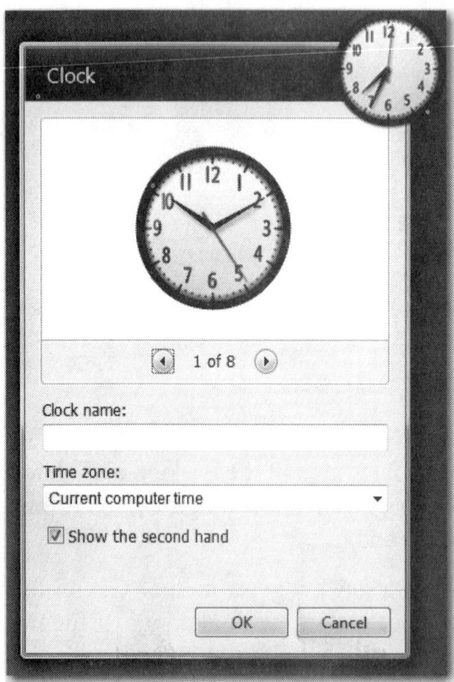

Exhibit 4-6: Changing the clock settings

Moving gadgets

To move a gadget, click its handle and drag it to where you want it. The handle is the bottom-most control button, and it looks like a grid of dots. When you drag a gadget, you need to grab its handle, because with some gadgets, clicking directly on them means that you want to do something, like write a new reminder note or open a news article.

Removing gadgets

To remove a gadget, click the Close button (the X button) to the right of it. You can also right-click the gadget and choose Close Gadget.

Do it!

B-1: Inspecting gadgets

Here's how	Here's why
1 Right-click the desktop and choose **Gadgets**	To open the Gadget Gallery

Step	Here's why
2 Double-click the clock gadget	It appears on the desktop, in the upper-right corner.
3 Add the calendar gadget	Double-click it. It shows today's date.
4 Close the Gadget Gallery	
5 Double-click the calendar	Anywhere around the date. It changes to a monthly calendar with today's date highlighted.
6 Point to the clock gadget	When you point to a gadget, its controls appear to the right of it.
Click the wrench icon, as shown	 The button that looks like a wrench opens the gadget's settings, as shown in Exhibit 4-6. Note the bottom control button that looks like a grid of dots. This is the handle by which you can drag the gadget to a new location.
7 Change the clock face to one of your choosing	Use the arrow buttons under the clock face in the settings dialog box.
8 Click **OK**	To close the settings and change the clock.
9 Right-click the clock face and choose **Always on top**	So that the clock will stay on top of open windows.
10 Point to the calendar and click the Larger size button, as shown	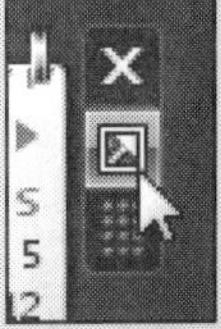 To see both calendars.
11 With the calendar gadget's buttons still visible, use the handle to drag the calendar to the lower-right area of the screen	The handle is at the bottom of the gadget's control buttons.
12 Right-click the calendar gadget and choose **Close gadget**	To close the calendar.
13 Point to the clock and then click its Close button	It's the X button in the gadget controls.

Topic C: System settings

Explanation

Windows 7 provides a number of configuration tools. Although some of them are too advanced for this course, we will cover some that you can use to customize your Windows 7 working environment to suit your needs and preferences. For example, you can change the color scheme and the desktop background.

The Control Panel

The Control Panel, shown in Exhibit 4-7, is a central location for tools that you use to customize and manage your Windows 7 computer. To open the Control Panel, click Start and choose Control Panel.

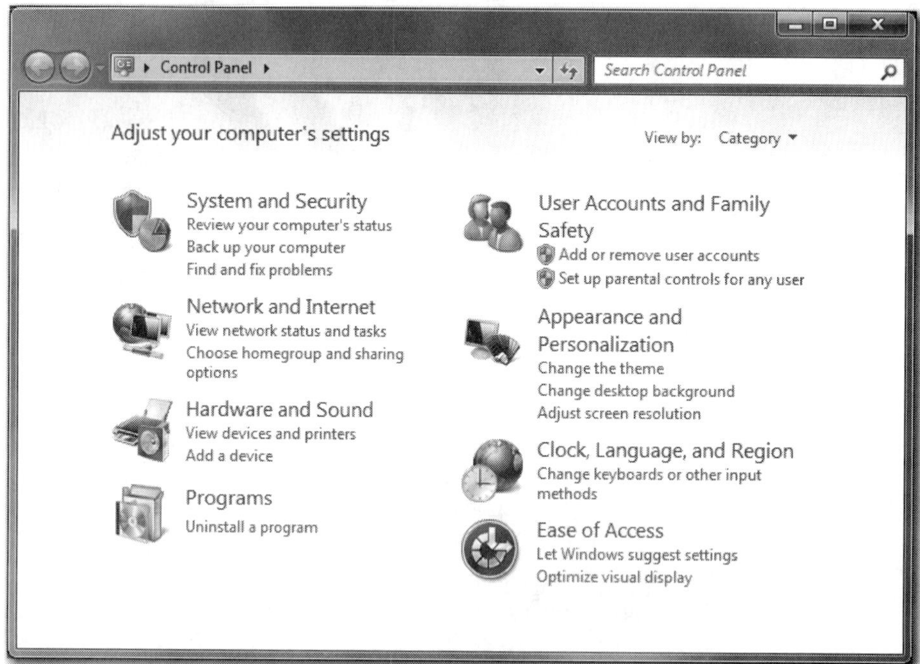

Exhibit 4-7: The Windows 7 Control Panel

Mouse properties

You can customize your mouse to suit your needs and work preferences. For example, if you are left-handed, you can configure the right button as the primary button, and the left button as the secondary button. You can then use the right button for double-clicking, dragging, and selecting, and use the left button for opening shortcut menus. You can also change the speed with which the mouse pointer moves across the screen.

To access the mouse properties, open the Control Panel, click Hardware and Sound, and click Mouse. The Mouse Properties dialog box, shown in Exhibit 4-8, contains five tabs, as described in the following table:

Tab	Use this tab to…
Buttons	Specify whether the mouse is set for right-hand or left-hand use. You can also set the double-click speed and activate ClickLock.
Pointers	Specify the appearance of your mouse pointer.
Pointer Options	Specify how you want the pointer to act on screen.
Wheel	Configure the click wheel settings, if your mouse has one.
Hardware	Set your mouse driver properties.

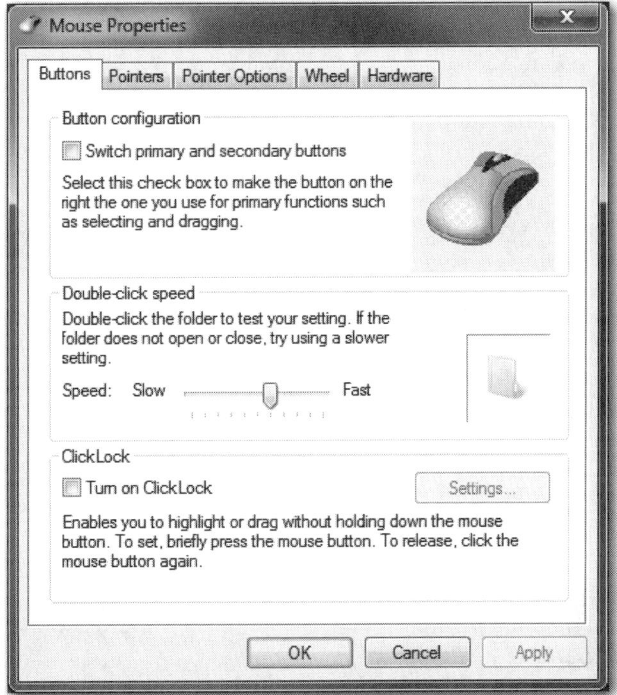

Exhibit 4-8: The Mouse Properties dialog box

Do it!

C-1: Setting mouse properties

Here's how	Here's why
1 Click **Start** and choose **Control Panel**	To open the Control Panel.
2 Click **Hardware and Sound**	
Under Devices and Printers, click **Mouse**	To open the Mouse Properties dialog box. The Buttons tab is displayed by default.
Observe the options	By default, the mouse is configured for right-handed use. The double-click speed is set about halfway between Slow and Fast.
3 Under "Double-click speed," drag the slider bar to the right	To increase the double-click speed.
To the right of the slider, double-click the yellow folder	To test the new double-click speed. If you double-click successfully, the folder opens (or closes if it is already open).
Reduce the double-click speed	Slow Fast To set it to a comfortable setting.
4 Activate the Pointers tab	You'll change the pointer scheme.
Under Scheme, from the list, select **Windows Inverted (large) (system scheme)**	This is the new pointer scheme.
Observe the Customize list	It displays the pointer shapes that will appear in various situations.
Click **Apply**	To apply the selected pointer scheme. The pointer shape is the same, but the pointer's color changes depending on the background, and it appears negatively translucent.
5 Change the pointer scheme back to **Windows Aero (system scheme)**	Select this scheme from the list and click Apply.
6 Activate the Pointer Options tab	You can change the speed of the pointer relative to the mouse movement. There are also several pointer visibility options.
7 Click **OK**	To close the Mouse Properties dialog box.

Keyboard properties

Explanation

You can also change the keyboard properties. To do so, open the Control Panel, click Ease of Access, and then click "Change how your keyboard works." This will open a page with several options, and at the bottom of this page is a link for Keyboard Settings. Click that link to open the Keyboard Properties dialog box, shown in Exhibit 4-9. This dialog box has two tabs: Speed and Hardware. The Hardware tab is used for advanced configuration options.

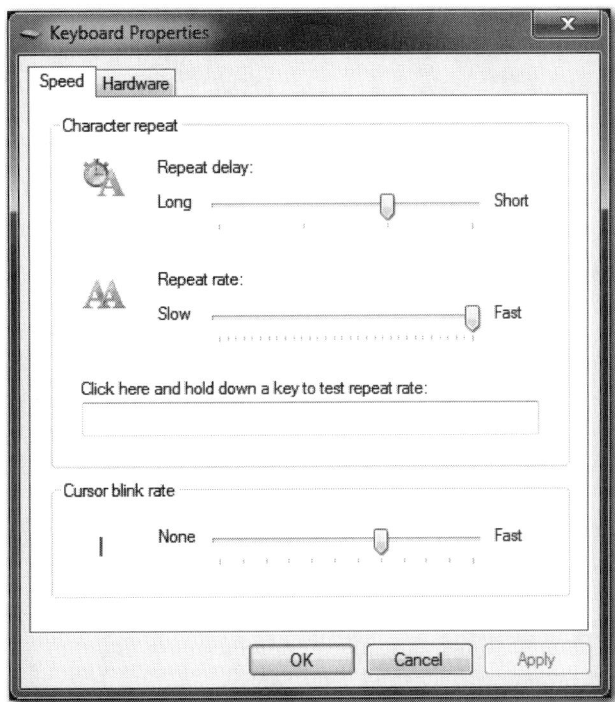

Exhibit 4-9: The Keyboard Properties dialog box

The options on the Speed tab are described in the following table.

Property	Description
Repeat delay	Specifies how long Windows waits before repeating a character whose key you're pressing down.
Repeat rate	Specifies how quickly a character is repeated when you hold down its key.
Cursor blink rate	Specifies the rate at which the insertion point blinks on the screen.

Do it!

C-2: Setting keyboard properties

Here's how	Here's why
1 In the Control Panel, click **Ease of Access**	
Click **Change how your keyboard works**	To see usability options for the keyboard.
Observe the options	Scroll down. At the bottom of the page, there are also links for changing the keyboard type and other keyboard settings.
2 Click **Keyboard settings**	To open the Keyboard Properties dialog box.
3 Under "Cursor blink rate," drag the slider bar all the way to the right	To increase the rate at which the cursor blinks. A sample blinking cursor is shown to the left of the slider bar to indicate the new blink rate.
4 Set the Cursor blink rate to a rate of your choice	
5 Click **OK**	To apply the settings and close the Properties dialog box.

Personalizing your computer

Explanation

You can change the desktop picture and colors as you please by using the Personalization settings in the Control Panel. To access these settings, shown in Exhibit 4-10, click Appearance and Personalization in the Control Panel, and then click Personalization. You can also right-click the desktop and choose Personalize to get to the same place.

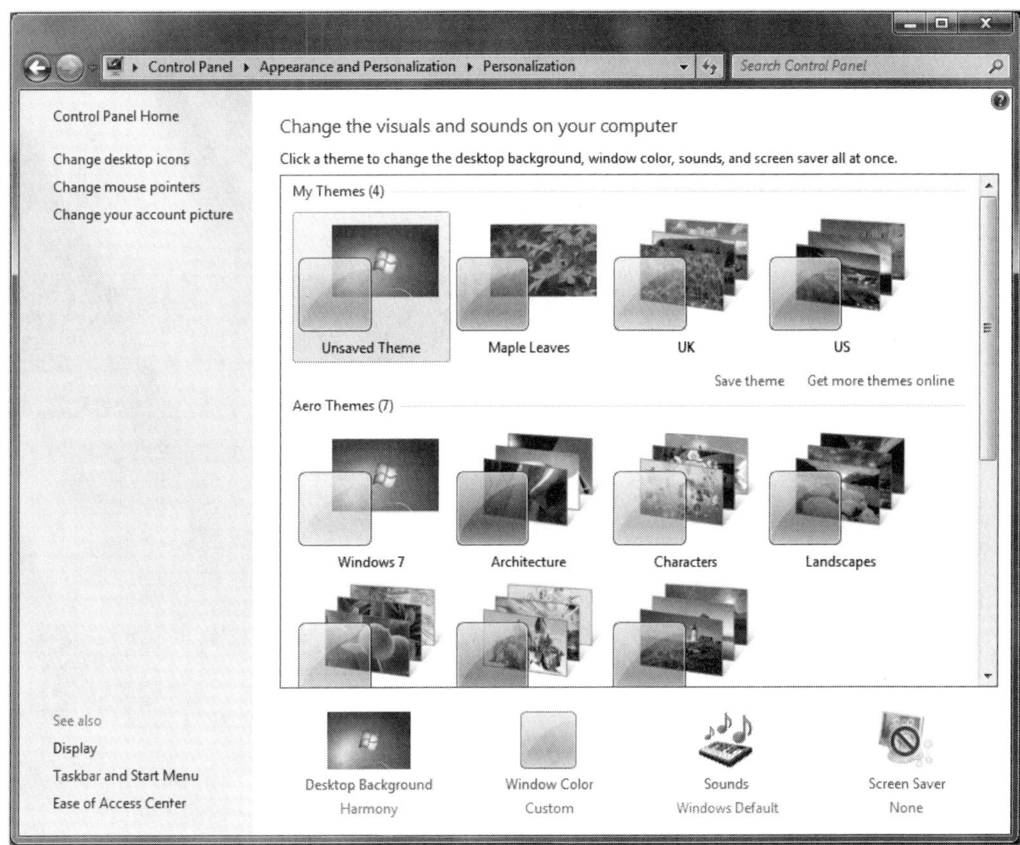

Exhibit 4-10: Personalization settings for visuals and sounds

The following table describes some of what you can do with the various Personalization settings.

Category	Use settings to...
Theme	Change the overall design of your system by using predefined combinations of background, sounds, colors, and icons.
Desktop Background	Add wallpaper or a background pattern to the desktop.
Window Color	Change the colors used for various window components.
Sounds	Choose the sound effects you hear when working with Windows.
Screen Saver	Activate and control a screen saver—a graphic that appears on your monitor when your computer is idle for a specified amount of time.

Changing the desktop background

You can change the desktop background, setting it to a color, pattern, or wallpaper of your choice. *Wallpaper* is a picture that appears on your desktop background. To modify the desktop background:

1. Click Start and choose Control Panel.
2. Click Appearance and Personalization and then click Personalization. You can also right-click an empty area of the desktop and choose Personalize to get to this step.
3. Click Desktop Background to display the options shown in Exhibit 4-11.
4. Select a picture category from the Picture Location list and then select the picture you want. You can also browse to a picture file you have saved elsewhere.
5. Click Save changes.

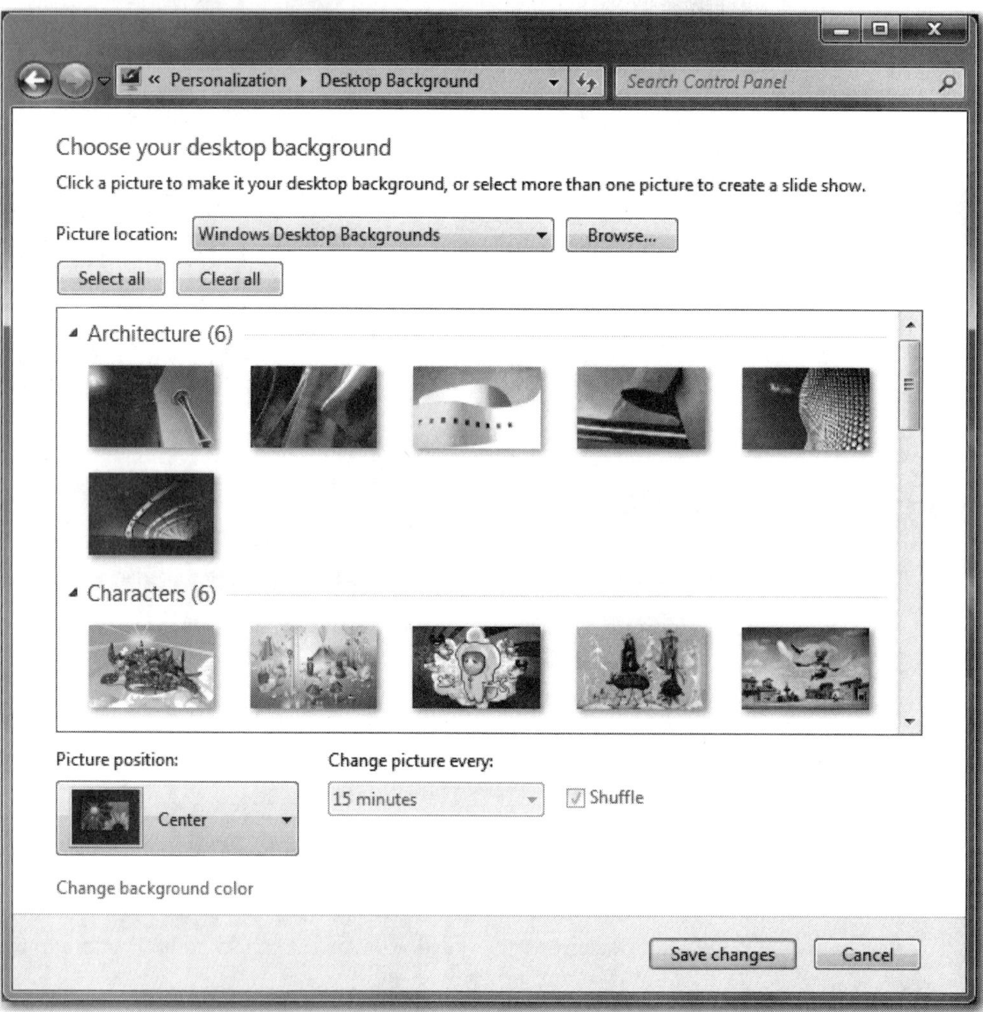

Exhibit 4-11: Selecting a background

Do it!

C-3: Choosing a new desktop background

Here's how	Here's why
1 Click [back button] three times	(In the Control Panel.) To return to the Control Panel home page.
2 Click **Appearance and Personalization**	
Click **Personalization**	
Click **Desktop Background**	
3 From the Picture Location list, select **Windows Desktop Backgrounds**	(If necessary.) You can choose wallpaper images from your Pictures folder, from sample wallpapers included with Windows, from the Public Pictures folder, or elsewhere.
Select any background	Scroll up—many backgrounds are available. The desktop changes right away so you can see how it will look.
4 Click **Save changes**	To accept the new background and return to the Personalization settings.

Screen savers

Explanation

A *screen saver* is an animation that appears on your monitor when your computer is idle for a specified period of time. Screen savers hide data on your screen from passersby. Furthermore, if the screen saver is set to display the logon screen when you resume work, you will need to log back on to turn off the screen saver. This setting adds security by locking your computer if you happen to step away longer than you expected.

To change your screen saver, open the Personalization page of the Control Panel and click Screen Saver. This opens the Screen Saver Settings dialog box, shown in Exhibit 4-12. From here you can choose the screen saver and specify how long the computer should be idle before the screen saver turns on. Some screen savers have additional settings you can change.

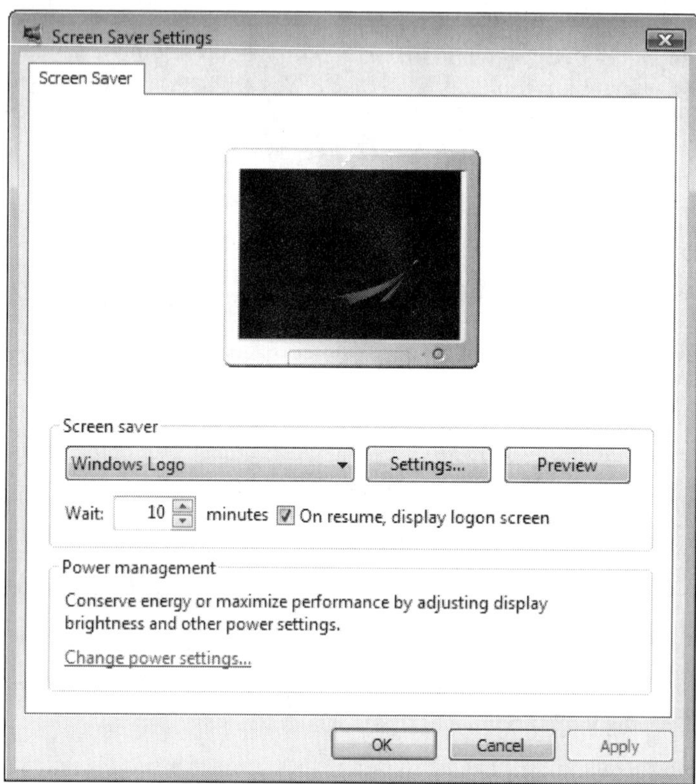

Exhibit 4-12: Screen Saver Settings

Power savings

Screen savers can add a very small measure of power savings if the screen saver displays mostly black. The Windows Logo and Starfield screen savers, for example, show a mostly black screen with a logo or moving "stars." It takes less energy to display black on your monitor than other colors.

Much greater savings come from turning off the monitor altogether. By default, Windows 7 is set to turn off the monitor after an idle period. Thus, if your screen saver runs for more than a few minutes, Windows 7 turns off the monitor so that it displays nothing.

Do it!

C-4: Choosing a screen saver

Here's how	Here's why
1 Click **Screen Saver**	(On the Personalization page of the Control Panel.) To open the Screen Saver Settings dialog box.
2 From the Screen saver list, select a screen saver	After a moment, a preview of the screen saver is shown in the preview "monitor" above the drop-down list.
Click **Preview**	The screen saver you selected is displayed full screen.
Move your mouse	The screen saver is deactivated.
3 Try another screen saver and then select your favorite	
4 Change the time interval to **15** minutes	After this interval, Windows will display the screen saver. You can change the time interval by clicking the up or down arrows on the Wait box or by typing a value in the box.
5 Check **On resume, display logon screen**	When checked, this setting requires you to log in when you return to your computer and want to turn off the screen saver.
Clear **On resume, display logon screen**	For convenience, you'll leave this option unchecked during class.
6 Click **OK**	To close the dialog box and save your choice.

Sound settings

Explanation

Most computers have a small system speaker at the very least, while many have a full set of speakers through which you can listen to music, movies, video clips, and even television broadcasts, depending on your system configuration. You can use the Control Panel to change the sounds your computer plays and the volume at which it plays them. If you have a sound card and a program installed to configure it, you have even greater control over the sounds your computer produces.

To access sound settings, click Sounds in the Personalization window. If you just want to change the volume, click the small speaker icon in the notification area of the taskbar and adjust the volume up or down (or mute the sound altogether).

Do it!

C-5: Configuring sound settings

Here's how	Here's why
1 In the Personalization window, click **Sounds**	To open the Sound dialog box.
Observe the Sounds tab	You can use these settings to change default system sounds.
2 In the Program Events list, select **Default Beep**	
Observe the Sounds list	The Windows Ding sound file is configured as the default beep.
3 Click **Test**	To listen to the sound.
4 From the Sounds list, select **Windows Notify.wav**	To select a different sound for the default beep.
Click **Test**	To listen to the sound. If you preferred this sound, you could leave it as the choice for the default beep.
5 Activate the Playback tab	
Observe the settings	You can select installed audio devices and configure them here. If the audio devices have their own configuration programs, you can configure them by using those programs instead.
6 Activate the Recording tab	
Observe the settings	You can configure input devices, such as microphones, on this tab.
7 Click **Cancel**	To close the Sound dialog box without applying or saving any changes, and return to the Control Panel.
8 Close the Control Panel and any open windows	
9 Click the speaker icon in the notification area and mute the sound	Click the speaker icon under the volume slider. Depending on your sound device, the volume shortcut will have other buttons besides the slider and the mute option.

Unit summary: Customizing the environment

Topic A In this topic, you customized your desktop and Start menu. You created a **shortcut** on the desktop and **pinned icons** to the Start menu and the taskbar. Then you deleted the shortcut from the desktop and put it in the Recycle Bin. You also unpinned and removed shortcuts from the Start menu.

Topic B In this topic, you learned about **Windows gadgets**. You learned how to add, move, and remove gadgets, and how to change their settings and properties.

Topic C In this topic, you customized some of your **system settings** by using the **Control Panel**. You set properties for your mouse and keyboard. Finally, you changed your desktop background, selected a new screen saver, and adjusted the sound.

Review questions

1 How do you change a gadget's settings?

2 What is the name of the list of recent locations and documents you see when you right-click or drag up on a taskbar button?

3 What is it called when you add a permanent shortcut to the Start menu? PIN to

4 Where can you find many tools for customizing system settings? Control Panel

5 Where do you find the dialog box that you use to change keyboard settings?

6 Why might you want to change the rate at which the insertion point blinks?

7 Why would you use a screen saver?

8 When you delete a shortcut, what happens to the original item that the shortcut pointed to? Stays The Same

9 Let's say you're left-handed and want to use the mouse to the left of your keyboard. You find it inconvenient that the primary mouse button is the mouse's left button. What can you do about this?

10 How do programs get added to the Start menu if you don't pin them there?

Independent practice activity

In this activity, you will add an icon to the taskbar and add, modify, and remove a gadget.

1 Pin the Calculator program to the taskbar.

2 Right-click the desktop and choose Personalize. Choose a new desktop background. Remove the screen saver. Close the Personalize window.

3 Open the Gadget Gallery. Add the Slide Show gadget to the desktop. Close the gallery.

4 Open the Slide Show options. From the folder list, select Sample Pictures. Change the interval between pictures to 5 seconds, and change the transition to Fade.

5 Close the options and watch the slide show for a few slides.

6 Remove the slideshow gadget from the desktop.

7 Un-mute the computer speakers.

8 Close all windows.

Unit 5

Internet Explorer 8

Unit time: 75 minutes

Complete this unit, and you'll know how to:

A Browse the World Wide Web by using Internet Explorer.

B Use the tabbed browsing feature in Internet Explorer.

C Conduct searches in Internet Explorer.

D Customize Internet Explorer.

E Access multimedia content and software on the Web.

Topic A: Web browsing

Explanation

In corporate and government environments, e-mail and the World Wide Web have become as indispensable as the telephone, and maybe more so. Internet access has become commonplace in homes, schools, libraries, coffee shops, and airports.

Internet software

The two most important pieces of software for Internet users are e-mail programs and Web browsers. *E-mail* programs allow you to send written messages and file attachments to anyone who has an e-mail address. Some e-mail programs are standalone applications, but Web-based mail is increasingly popular, partially because your mail is stored online and you can get to it from any computer.

A *Web browser* is a program that provides a graphical view of the World Wide Web. Web browsers give you access to Web sites, which are composed of *Web pages*. A Web page may contain text, graphics, animations, sounds, movies, and a variety of other interactive elements. A Web browser makes it easy to navigate or "surf" the Web, download items, print Web pages, and mark your favorite pages for easy access.

Internet Explorer 8

Internet Explorer is the most popular Web browser, and the version included with Windows 7 is Internet Explorer 8. Internet Explorer is installed automatically when you install Windows 8 on your computer. Before you can use Internet Explorer to browse the Web, your system must be connected to the Internet. When you are connected to the Internet, you are said to be *online*.

Internet connections

At work or at home, going online may require only turning on your computer, because many organizations and home networks automatically connect to the Internet. The network connection usually comes from an *Internet service provider*, or ISP. Home connections often get Internet access over the phone line via DSL (Digital Subscriber Line) or through the same kind of cable that's used for cable TV.

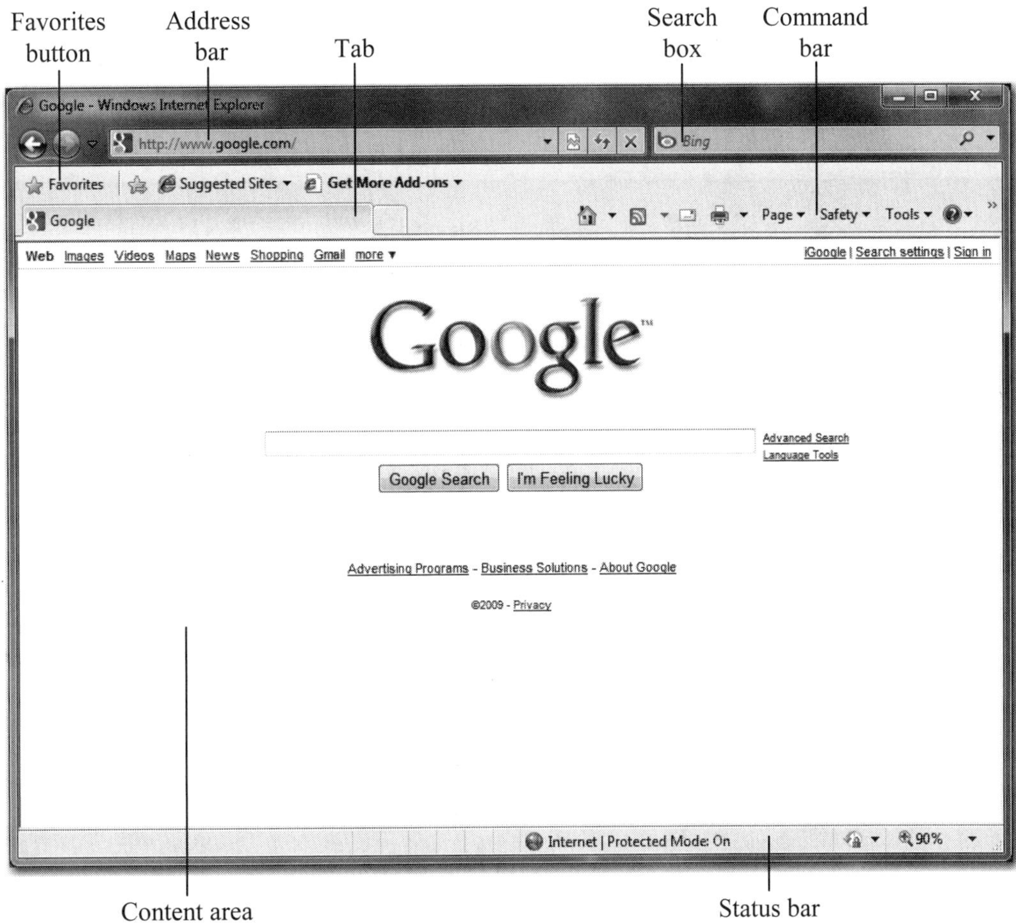

Exhibit 5-1: The components of the Internet Explorer window

The Internet Explorer window

To start Internet Explorer, click Start and choose All Programs, Internet Explorer, or click the Internet Explorer icon on the taskbar. When Internet Explorer opens, you'll see that the browser interface (shown in Exhibit 5-1) contains some components with which you are already familiar from working with other programs: a title bar, an Address bar, a Search box, and a toolbar.

Internet Explorer's window components are described in the following table.

Component	Use to...
Navigation buttons	Move backward and forward through pages in a single Web site or between multiple Web sites. To the right of the forward button, there is a down-arrow that displays the History list.
Address bar	Enter the address of a Web page you want to view. Web addresses are called *Uniform Resource Locators* (URLs). They are in the familiar "www" and "dot com" format that you see everywhere these days.
Search box	Search for information on the Web by using Microsoft's Bing search capabilities.
Favorites Center	Display your Favorites list, History list, and RSS (Really Simple Syndication) feeds list.
Tabs	View multiple Web sites without opening multiple Internet Explorer windows. Each tab shows the name of the Web page it's displaying.
Command bar	Access common commands, including returning to your home page, adding RSS feeds, printing pages, and changing privacy and other settings.
Information Bar	Approve certain actions that some Web sites may require, such as opening pop-ups or downloading programs, ActiveX controls, and plug-ins. (The Information Bar appears at the top of the content area only when necessary and is not shown in Exhibit 5-1.)
Content area	View Web pages.
Status bar	View messages relating to Internet Explorer's operation.

Do it!

A-1: Exploring the Internet Explorer interface

Here's how	Here's why
1 On the taskbar, click 	This is the taskbar icon for Internet Explorer. You can also open it from the Start menu.
2 Observe the content area	The content area displays the current Web page.
3 Observe the Address bar	The text you see is the address for the current Web page. As you navigate to other Web pages, the Address bar will display the address of each page.
4 Observe the Search box	 Bing is the default search engine for Internet Explorer 8. You can type a word or phrase to search for related information on the Web.
5 Click Favorites	To open the Favorites Center. You can display your Favorites list, your RSS feeds, and your History list in this pane.
Click Favorites again	To close the Favorites Center.
6 Observe the Command bar	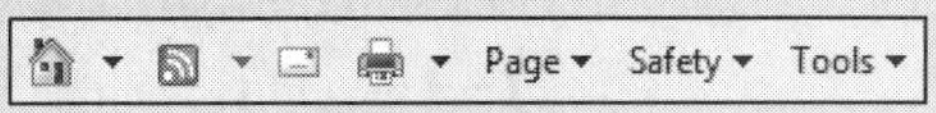 Click these buttons to return to your home page, access RSS feed information, print pages, and change Internet Explorer settings.
7 Observe the status bar	(At the bottom of the window.) The status bar provides information about the current Web page, as well as current Internet Explorer options.

Basic Web navigation

Explanation

Before you start using Internet Explorer to surf the Web, it is helpful to understand more about hyperlinks and URLs. These are the most basic navigational elements of the Web environment.

Hyperlinks

Hyperlinks are clickable connections between Web pages. A hyperlink can be a word or phrase, an icon, a picture, a button, or an animated element on a Web page. When you point to a hyperlink, the pointer changes to a pointing hand, as shown in Exhibit 5-2. At the same time, the Internet Explorer status bar shows the URL associated with the hyperlink to which you are pointing.

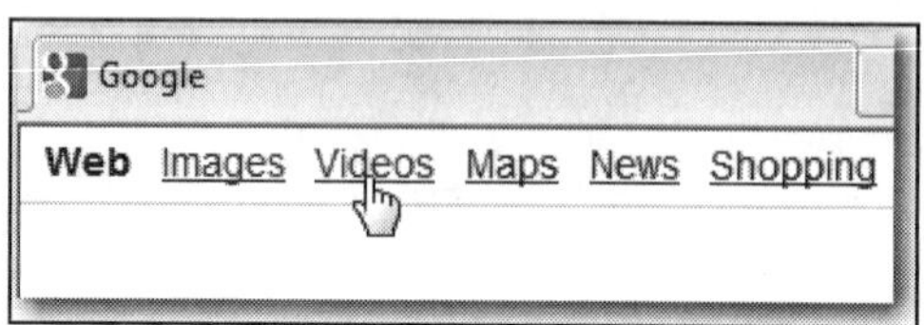

Exhibit 5-2: The pointing hand indicates a hyperlink

A hyperlink can take you just about anywhere on the Web: to another location on the same Web page; to another Web page on the same Web site; or to a different Web site altogether. A hyperlink can even trigger a file download or cause another program to open on your computer. Web page designers use Hypertext Markup Language (HTML) to specify the URL, or target address, for each hyperlink.

Text-based hyperlinks are often underlined or displayed in a different color than the rest of the text on the Web page. Graphics-based hyperlinks can be icons, logos, buttons, photographs, and so on. On more sophisticated Web pages, pointing to a hyperlink can reveal other hyperlinks or change what's displayed in other areas of the Web page. When you're not sure where the hyperlinks are located on a Web page, you can move your mouse pointer around the screen; when the pointer changes to a pointing hand, you have found a hyperlink.

URLs and the Address bar

Clicking a hyperlink is just one way to access a specific URL. If you already know the URL of the Web page you want to visit, you can type it in the Address bar and press Enter (or click the arrow button). When you work with the Address bar, it is helpful to understand the structure of a URL.

URLs use a standard syntax:

```
protocol://website/resource
```

- `protocol` is the type of Internet language used to open the selected resource. Common languages are `http` (for Web pages), `file`, `ftp`, `telnet`, and `gopher`.
- `website` is the name of the Web site that contains the selected resource. Web site host names often have a prefix of `www` and a suffix of `com`, `net`, `org`, `gov`, `biz`, `info`, or something similar. In between is the domain name, which often matches a company's name or a product name.
- `resource` is the path and name of the specific file you're looking for. For many URLs, the resource is just a slash (/).

When you enter a URL in the Address bar and press Enter, Internet Explorer sends a request to your ISP's host computer to search the Internet for the URL you typed. It is not necessary to specify the protocol in a URL—the correct protocol will be used based on the Web address you enter. For example, if you wanted to visit the Microsoft Windows Web page, you would type `www.microsoft.com/windows` (which you will hear as "www dot Microsoft dot com slash windows") in the Address bar. Internet Explorer automatically inserts the protocol `http://` after you press Enter.

At the end of the Address bar is a button that changes depending on what you're doing:

- If you're typing a URL, the button is a right-pointing arrow. This is the Go button, which will take you to the URL you typed in the Address bar.
- When you're viewing a Web page, the button turns into two arrows pointing in a circular direction. This is the Refresh button, and it will reload the page you're viewing if you want to see if content has changed or been updated, or if the Web page isn't displayed properly.

The AutoComplete feature

Internet Explorer's AutoComplete feature makes it easy to enter previously visited URLs in the Address bar. When you begin typing the URL, the Address bar displays a drop-down list that contains previously visited URLs that begin with the same characters. As you continue to type, the list changes to match what you've entered. When you see the URL you want to access, you can stop typing and select it from the drop-down list. This feature is useful when you can't remember the exact URL but you know you've typed it before.

Do it!

A-2: Using hyperlinks and the Address bar

Here's how	Here's why
1 Slowly move the pointer over the Web page until you find a hyperlink	To see how the mouse pointer changes as you move it across a Web page and over a hyperlink.
Observe the pointer	Images It changes to a pointing hand, indicating that you are pointing to a hyperlink.
Observe the left end of the status bar	The URL associated with the hyperlink you are pointing to appears on the left side of the status bar.
2 Point to other hyperlinks	You'll notice that hyperlinks can be text or graphics.
3 Click a link	To go to the link's target Web page. Notice that the URL for the new page appears in the Address bar.
4 Click	To go back to the Web page you were viewing when you started this activity.
5 Click	To move forward to the Web page you just left. This button is available only after you've clicked the Back button.
6 Click	(On the Command bar.) To return to your home page. You are now back where you started.
7 Click in a blank area of the Address bar	To select the text.
Type **www.msn.com**	This is the Microsoft Network home page.
Press ENTER	To go to the MSN site.
In the Address bar, observe the URL	Internet Explorer automatically inserted the protocol (`http://`) into the URL.
8 In the Address bar, type **www.nasa.gov**	To enter the URL for NASA's Web site.
At the end of the Address bar, click	(The Go button.) To go to the NASA Web site. You could also press Enter.
9 At the end of the Address bar, click	(The Refresh button.) To reload the Web page and refresh the content. If the Web page is static, without a lot of graphics or banner ads, you might not notice much of a difference.

10	Edit the Address bar to read **www.m**	Internet Explorer displays the address AutoComplete list.
	From the Address list, select **http://www.msn.com**	The AutoComplete feature frees you from having to type the entire URL for a site you have visited recently. This feature can be helpful for long URLs.

The History list

Explanation

The Internet Explorer History list keeps track of all the sites you've visited within the past 20 days. To display the list of recent pages, click the down-arrow next to the Forward button. To display the full History list, do any of the following:

- Select History from the list of recent pages.
- Press Ctrl+Shift+H.
- Click the Favorites button and then click the History tab.

By using the drop-down list below the History tab, you can choose how you want to sort the items in the list—alphabetically by site, by date, by frequency of visits, and so on.

To close the History list, click the Close button or press Ctrl+Shift+H.

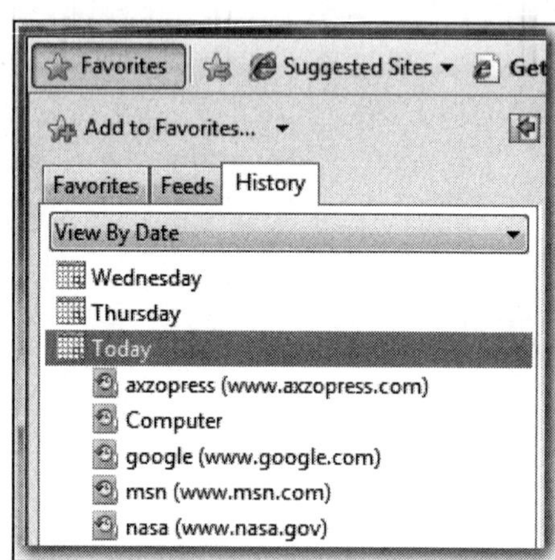

Exhibit 5-3: A History list

Do it!

A-3: Working with the History list

Here's how	Here's why
1 Click the Recent Pages button, as shown	(To the right of the Forward button.) To display the list of recent pages. You can see the sites you've visited during class.
2 Select a site from the list	To go to that site again.
3 Press CTRL + SHIFT + H	To open the History list in the Favorites Center. You could also click Favorites and then click the History tab.
4 Click the down-arrow to the right of View By Date and select **View By Site**	To sort the History list alphabetically by site name.
Select a site in the list	To navigate to that site.
5 Click	To return to your home page.
6 Close the History list	Press Ctrl+Shift+H, or click the Close button in the upper-right corner of the pane.

Topic B: Tabbed browsing

Explanation

Tabs let you open several Web sites in the same browser window. You can easily flip between these pages by clicking their tabs.

Tabs

Without tabs, you would have to open several instances of the browser to get the same effect. While you can visit multiple sites simultaneously either way, tabs make for a less-cluttered window environment. You have the option to turn off tabbed browsing.

With tabbed browsing, you can:

- Open and close tabs with a single click.
- Save tab groups as Favorites.
- Create a home group so that several tabs open when you start the browser or click the Home button.
- See a page showing small versions of all open tabs.

To open a new tab, click the small blank tab to the right of the open tab(s). The new tab will open to a blank page. Exhibit 5-4 shows tabs and related tools. To close the active tab (unless it's the only tab), click the Close button on the right side of it.

Exhibit 5-4: Tabs and tab tools

The tab list

Depending on the size of your browser window, up to about 10 tabs can be visible at a time. If you open more tabs than can be shown at once, you'll have to use the tab list to switch to the tabs you can't see. To open the tab list, click the Tab List button, which is the down-arrow just to the left of the tabs. You can then see all of the opened tabs and the full titles, and select a tab to view.

Quick Tabs

Use the Quick Tabs feature to see a miniature version of every tab you have open. This information sometimes takes a while to load, and it isn't nearly as fast as choosing tabs from the tab list. To see these thumbnail Web pages, click the Quick Tabs button, to the left of the Tab List button.

Tab groups

A tab group is a set of open tabs. You can save tab groups in your Favorites. For instance, if you are deciding which movie to rent, you might typically open Netflix, Roger Ebert's review site, the Rotten Tomatoes review site, and the Internet Movie Database (IMDB) site. You can open all of these, and then save that tab group in your Favorites with the name Movies. When you do so, a folder named Movies appears in your Favorites list. Click the arrow to the right of this folder to open all of the pages at once, on separate tabs. You can also expand the folder and open just one of the pages.

Setting home page tabs

You can set your home page to any page, including a file on your own computer. You can also have a home tab group, so that several tabs open when you start the browser or click the Home button. To change your home page, browse to the desired page, click the down-arrow next to the Home button, and choose Change Home Page. You will be offered two or three options, depending on whether you have one or more tabs open:

- **Use this as your only home page** — Replaces any other home page(s) with the active page, but not any other tabs that might be open.
- **Add this page to your home page tabs** — Adds the active page to any other pages you have. Pages will appear on tabs when you start the browser or click the Home button.
- **Use current tab set as your home page** — Is available only if you have more than one tab open. Replaces a page or pages with the current group of tabs.

To remove a tab from your home pages, click the down-arrow next to the Home button and choose Remove. Then choose the tab you want to remove, or choose Remove All. If you remove all of the pages, your home page will be blank.

Exhibit 5-5: Internet Options, showing multiple home page tabs

To see a list of your home pages, and to manually add, remove, and rearrange them, click Tools and choose Internet Options. This opens the Internet Options dialog box, shown in Exhibit 5-5. At the top of the General tab, there's a list of home pages.

Setting a default for new tabs

New tabs open a blank page by default. If you would rather have new tabs open your home page, you can set that option, and many others, in the Tabbed Browsing Settings dialog box, shown in Exhibit 5-6. Here's how:

1. Click Tools and choose Internet Options.
2. On the General tab, under Tabs, click Settings.
3. Click the button under the label "When a new tab is opened, open:" to display a list, and then select the desired action.
4. Click OK twice to close the dialog boxes.

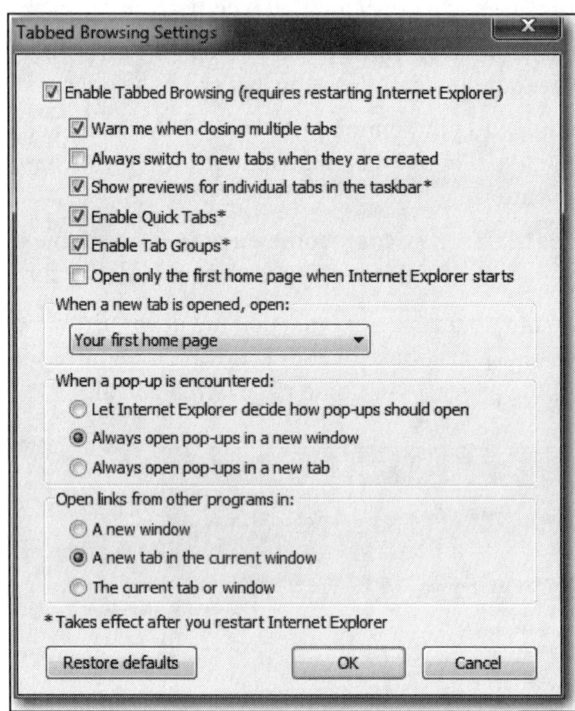

Exhibit 5-6: Settings for tabbed browsing

Use the tabbed browsing settings, shown in Exhibit 5-6, to adjust the behavior of the tabs and to enable or disable certain features. For instance, you can have the browser open only the first home page of your home group when the browser starts. When this option is checked, you have to click the Home button to load the remaining tabs in the home group.

Disabling tabbed browsing

If you want to disable tabbed browsing altogether, just clear the Enable Tabbed Browsing checkbox at the top of the Tabbed Browsing Settings dialog box.

Do it!

B-1: Opening and switching between tabs

Here's how	Here's why
1 Click the New Tab button, as shown	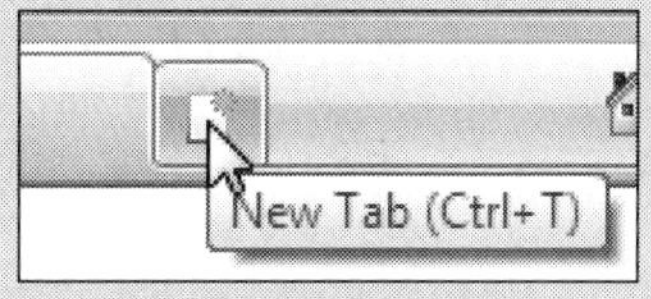 New Tab (Ctrl+T) To open a new tab.
2 In the Address bar, enter **www.microsoft.com**	To visit Microsoft's Web page.
3 Activate the MSN.com tab	Each tab displays a separate Web site.
4 Activate the Microsoft Corporation tab	You could switch back and forth between tabs to compare information on different Web pages.
5 Open a new tab to any site you want	You should have three tabs open now.
6 Click the Tab List button, as shown	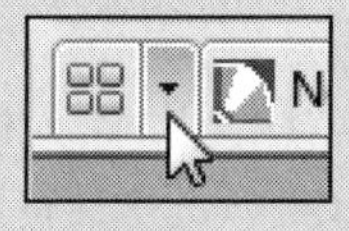 To display a list of open tabs.
7 Click 	(The Quick Tabs button is to the left of the Tab List button.) This feature shows you a small version of each tab you have open.
8 Click any page to switch to it	

Topic C: Web searching

Explanation

In Internet Explorer, you can conduct searches directly from the toolbar. Internet Explorer 8 uses Windows Bing by default, but you can choose a different search engine, such as Google or Yahoo!. You can also add specific site searches, such as Amazon books, eBay auctions, or Monster jobs.

Basic searching methods

To use the basic search function, enter a word or phrase in the search text box in the upper-right corner of the browser window; then press Enter or click the magnifying-glass button. If you want the search results to open on a new tab, press the Alt key as you press Enter.

To move the cursor to the search box by using the keyboard, press Ctrl+E. You can also search from the Address bar by entering the word "find" followed by your search terms.

Search tips

The following tips apply to most search sites. Some details might vary, but the features described here are usually available.

- Case doesn't matter. "Buffalo Bill" will return the same results as "buffalo bill" or "BUFFalo bill."
- Use quotation marks to keep words and phrases together. The search will return results with the exact words in the order you specified. Otherwise, you'll get pages that have your search terms, but not necessarily in the order you entered them in. Case still doesn't matter, even in quotation marks.
- If you misspell a term or two, you'll still see results, but most search engines will suggest a correct spelling. If you search for a business named Ken's Kakes, you'll be asked if you really meant Ken's Cakes.
- Sometimes running a simple search on a term or two will get you the results you want. If you're getting swamped with results, however, or getting too few results, you can click Advanced. The Advanced options offer you ways to refine your search to get more useful results.
- Put a minus sign (-) in front of terms you want to exclude from the search (do not put a space between the minus sign and the word). Sites that contain this term will not be shown in the results, even if they contain the other search terms.

Do it!

C-1: Running a basic search

Here's how	Here's why
1 Press CTRL + E	To put the insertion point in the Bing search box.
2 Enter **cardinals blue jays**	You'll search on these terms.
3 Press ↵ ENTER	To run the search. You could also click the magnifying-glass icon to the right of the search box.
Observe the results	Most sites are about baseball.
4 In the search box, add **-baseball** and **-season**	(Don't remove the current terms.) To eliminate sites with the words "baseball" and "season."
Press ↵ ENTER	
Observe the results	More of the sites are about birds instead of baseball.

More searching methods

Explanation

Although the browser's search box is convenient, you might be more comfortable opening a search-engine Web site and starting your search from there. Doing this also gives you access to any special features on the site that wouldn't be available from the search box in Internet Explorer.

Google and other search engines

Google is one of the most popular search engines—so popular that "to Google" has become a verb. The following section refers specifically to Google, shown in Exhibit 5-7, but many of the features described here can be found on any major search site, such as Yahoo! or Lycos.

Exhibit 5-7: Google is one of the most popular search engines

Google services

Ninety percent of the time, a regular search is all you'll need, but the other Google services can be very useful because they greatly narrow the type of sites that are searched. You can click these options before or after you've done the search: Images, Videos, Maps, News, and Shopping. You can see more services by clicking the "more" link. Some of these services have "Beta" in the title, meaning that they are early versions, Google is still refining them, and they'll probably change.

Here are a few other fun things about Google:

- There are more services than the ones listed above. Click the "more" link to check them out. For instance, you can sign up to be alerted via e-mail when given terms show up with a certain frequency on certain types of sites.
- Google translates. If you get promising results in a language other than English, you might get a "Translate this page" link. The translation might not be perfect, but you'll get the gist of it. You can also search in and translate to other languages. Click Language Tools by the search field to see your options.
- You can do calculations and conversions. Enter a calculation, and Google returns an answer. You can include constants; for instance, entering "pi*2" will give you 6.28318531. You can enter things like "teaspoons in a cup" or "10 kilometers in miles," and Google will return what it thinks you want to know.

Do it!

C-2: Using Google

Here's how	Here's why
1 Go to **www.google.com**	In Internet Explorer.
2 In the search box, enter **pi * 3 squared**	
Press ENTER	To perform a calculation. Google will parse the English and the numeric terms and guess at what you want. The answer appears, along with a link to search for pages with these terms.
3 Edit the search box to read **Square feet in an acre** and press ENTER	To see how many square feet are in an acre.
4 Above the Google search box, click **News**	
5 Enter terms related to a news subject that interests you and press ENTER	
6 Above the Google search box, click **Maps**	To open Google Maps.
Enter your home address and press ENTER	To see a street map of your neighborhood.
Use the zoom/pan tool to zoom in and out on your neighborhood	
7 Above the Google search box, click **More** and then **Even More**	
Observe the various services and products	Explore any that interest you, as time allows.
8 Close all open windows	

Topic D: Customization

Explanation

Most people who use the Web regularly find themselves returning to the same handful of Web sites. These Web sites usually include preferred search engines, work- or school-related sites, news sources, and Web pages of personal interest. Use the Favorites feature in Internet Explorer to maintain a list of the sites you frequently use. Exhibit 5-8 shows the Favorites list.

Managing your Favorites

To add an entry to your Favorites list, first go to the Web page in Internet Explorer. Then click Favorites and Add to Favorites. This opens the Add a Favorite dialog box, with which you can assign a name for this favorite (if the default title isn't sufficient) and choose the folder in which to store it. You can also open the Add Favorites dialog box by right-clicking an empty area of the selected Web page and choosing Add to Favorites. The Add to Favorites Bar button (a star with a green arrow) will add the site to the Favorites bar.

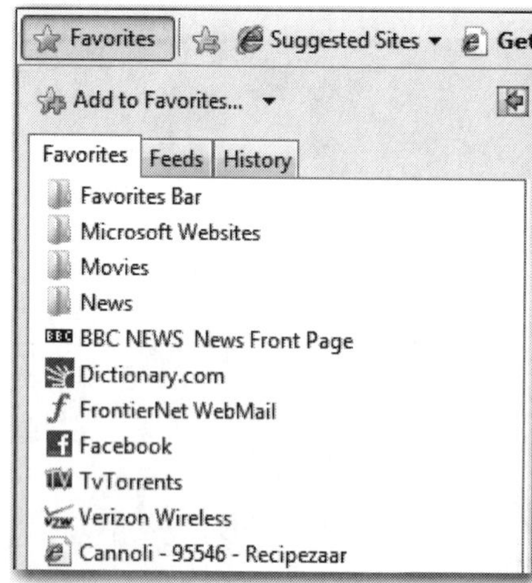

Exhibit 5-8: A sample Favorites list

To delete an entry from the Favorites list, open the Favorites Center dialog box. Then right-click the entry and choose Delete from the shortcut menu.

Do it!

D-1: Working with the Favorites list

Here's how	Here's why
1 If necessary, close all open tabs except one	
2 Go to **www.yahoo.com**	
Observe the content window	The Yahoo! page appears. Yahoo! is one of the most popular Web search engines. You will add Yahoo! to your Favorites list.

	Here's how	Here's why
3	Click [Favorites] and click **Add to Favorites...**	To open the Add a Favorite dialog box.
4	Display the **Create in** list	You can create the favorite in the Favorites folder (the default) or another folder in the list.
	Select **Favorites**	To close the list.
5	Click **New Folder**	To open the Create a Folder dialog box.
	Type **Search Engines**	To name the new folder. Internet Explorer will create it as a subfolder of the Favorites folder.
	Click **Create**	To create a folder named "Search Engines" and close the dialog box.
6	Observe the Add a Favorite dialog box	The Search Engines folder appears in the Create in list.
	Click **Add**	To add the Yahoo! page to the Search Engines folder.
7	Click [Favorites]	To display the Favorites list. The Search Engines folder is now included.
	Click the Favorites tab	If necessary.
	Click **Search Engines**	To expand the folder. There's the Yahoo! Web site you saved in this folder.
	Press ESC	To close the Favorites list. You could also click the title bar or a blank area of the Web page.
8	Visit **www.google.com**	
	Add it to the Search Engines folder in the Favorites list	Click Favorites and then click Add to Favorites. Select Search Engines from the Create in list. Click Add.
9	Open the Favorites Center	
	Expand **Search Engines**	(If necessary.) Google is listed along with Yahoo! in this folder.
10	Point to Search Engines and then click [→]	To open both Yahoo! and Google on new tabs. This button opens the folder in a new tab group.
11	Open **www.nytimes.com**	
	Click [☆]	The site is added to the Favorites bar.
12	Close all tabs except for the New York Times tab	

Privacy protection

Explanation

Because computer security is so important these days, and identify theft is on the rise, it's important to take care when using the Web, especially if you're sharing a computer with another user. One way to help protect yourself is to clear any personal information you've entered while using Internet Explorer to prevent criminals from taking advantage of customization features to steal your personal information.

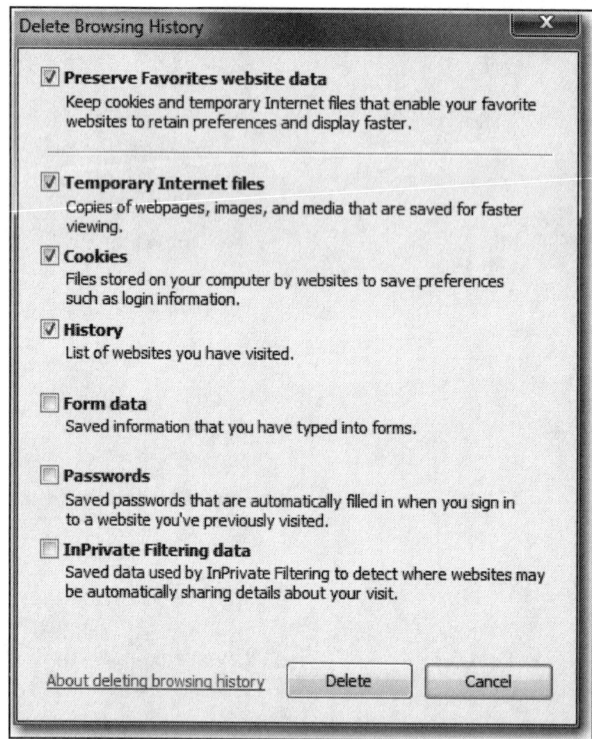

Exhibit 5-9: Delete Browsing History dialog box

To clear personal information, click the Safety button and choose Delete Browsing History to open the dialog box shown in Exhibit 5-9. You can use this dialog box to delete more than the browsing history. The dialog box describes the kinds of data you can remove. You can delete each type of information separately, or you can delete all types at the same time. Keep in mind that once you delete this information, you might be asked to supply personal information again the next time you visit a Web site where you've already entered it.

Do it!

D-2: Clearing your browser history

Here's how	Here's why
1 Click **Safety** and choose **Delete Browsing History...**	To open the Delete Browsing History dialog box.
2 Confirm that **Preserve Favorites website data** is checked	
Check **Form Data**	(Temporary Internet files, Cookies, and History should already be checked.) To confirm that you want to delete these things.
3 Click **Delete**	The dialog box closes and the data is deleted.

RSS feeds

Explanation

RSS stands for, among other things, Really Simple Syndication. It allows a Web site to alert you to new or updated content. For instance, the RSS feed from a world news site might send the latest headlines. You can often customize which updates you receive by subscribing to the results of a search.

RSS feeds are not limited to news headlines. Often Web logs, or *blogs*, offer this service. RSS feeds can download as little as a notification of changes with accompanying links, or as much as full articles, pictures, and sound and video files. The updating occurs behind the scenes, as you're doing other things.

Subscribing to RSS feeds

To receive an RSS feed from a site, you need to subscribe. When a site offers RSS feeds, the Feeds button lights up—that is, changes from gray to orange. To subscribe to an RSS feed:

1. Open a Web site that offers RSS feeds. The Feeds button (to the right of the Home button) will light up (become orange).
2. Click the Feeds button. If more than one is feed available, a page opens, showing you the latest updates.
3. If the site allows it, you can enter search terms to customize your feed.
4. At the top of the page, click "Subscribe to this feed."
5. Enter a name or leave the default, and then click Subscribe.

After you subscribe to a feed, you can see a summary of the updates in your Favorites list. Just click the Favorites button, click Feeds, and click the feed you want to see. To the right of each feed title, there is a button you can click to immediately check for updates.

Unsubscribing

To unsubscribe from a feed, right-click it in the Feeds list and choose Delete. Click OK to confirm the deletion and the removal of associated content.

Do it!

D-3: Adding an RSS news feed

Here's how	Here's why
1 Click [Feeds button]	The Feeds button is to the right of the Home button on the Command bar.
2 At the top of the page, click **Subscribe to this feed**	To open the feed subscription dialog box.
3 Observe the Create in list	This feed will be saved in the Feeds list.
4 Click **Subscribe**	
5 Click [Favorites]	To display the Favorites Center.
Click the **Feeds** tab	To display the list of feeds you have subscribed to.
6 Click **NYT > Home Page**	To view the current content of this feed.

Topic E: Multimedia content

Explanation

Audio content can include music, speeches, lectures, news stories, meetings, animal sounds, or even pronunciation examples from an online dictionary. While some of the audio content on the Web is intended for personal enjoyment, much of it provides valuable information that you can use on the job or in school.

Video content can include news stories, company presentations, or online courses through a training company or a college. Videos on the Web are usually highly compressed to save transmission time and space. Thus, the quality is not nearly as good as television, DVD, or VCR video technologies.

Windows Media Player

When you click a link for audio or video content, by default Internet Explorer tries to play it in Windows Media Player (WMP). Some audio and video files won't play in WMP and require a separate player, such as RealPlayer or QuickTime, that you must download from the Web.

Exhibit 5-10: Windows Media Player

A typical version of WMP is shown in Exhibit 5-10, and like most CD players, VCRs, and DVD players, it has some standard buttons that you can use to navigate through the video and audio. Typically the buttons will look like those in the following table.

Button	Description
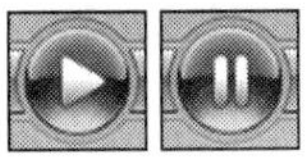	Click to play the content, or pause the playing. When content is playing, the Play button turns into the Pause button.
	Click the button to go to the previous track or chapter. Hold down the button to reverse or rewind.
	Click the button to go to the next track or chapter. Hold down the button to fast-forward.
	Click to stop playing content.
	Click to mute the sound. When the sound is muted, there's a red X to the right of this icon.
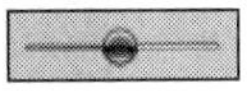	Drag to change the volume.
	Click to turn the repeat function on and off. Two arrows means that content will repeat.
	Click to shuffle the play order.
	(Above the control buttons.) Indicates the current position in the content; click or drag to move to a different position in the content.

You'll probably find some content that you'll want to download to your computer so you can play it any time in Windows Media Player. However, you will typically find it difficult or impossible to download commercial and copyrighted multimedia content.

Much of the audio and video content you'll find on the Web will play in a version of WMP embedded in the Web page. Sometimes Internet Explorer will open a separate WMP window.

Do it!

E-1: Playing audio content

Here's how	Here's why
1 In the Address bar, enter **encarta.msn.com**	(Do not add "www" to this URL.) To access the MSN Encarta online encyclopedia. While the full Encarta service is available by paid subscription, some content is available free or for limited-time access.
2 Under the MSN Encarta heading, click **More** and choose **Multimedia**	To open the Multimedia Center.
3 Click **Sounds**	To expand the Sounds category.
4 Click **Performing Arts**	To expand the Performing Arts category.
5 Select **Music**	To see a list of options in the right pane.
6 Select a piece of music without an asterisk	(Those with asterisks require a login to play.) To play it in WMP. The music should start after just a few seconds.
7 If necessary, scroll down the page	
Observe the WMP window embedded in the Web page	You might not see all the buttons you'd see in a full WMP window, but you can use the Play button to play the piece again, and you can control the volume. Often the screen will display patterns while the music is playing.
8 Click	To play the selection again.

Playing videos

Explanation

Like sound files, video files will often play in a media player embedded in the Web browser, as shown in Exhibit 5-11. Other times, you can download the video to your computer and play it separately in Windows Media Player.

Exhibit 5-11: Windows Media Player embedded in Internet Explorer

Do it!

E-2: Playing video content

Here's how	Here's why
1 At the top of the page, under the MSN Encarta heading, click **More** and choose **Multimedia**	To return to the Multimedia Center.
2 Click **Videos**	To expand the Videos category.
3 Click **Life Science**	
Select **Birds**	To display video content selections about birds.
4 Select a video on the right	To play it in WMP.
Select the appropriate connection speed	The higher your speed, the larger the video image and the better the quality. Also, the speed of your Internet connection will affect your ability to move back and forth through the content.
5 Close Internet Explorer	
Close all open windows	

Unit summary: Internet Explorer 8

Topic A In this topic, you browsed the World Wide Web by using **Internet Explorer**. You learned about the components of the Internet Explorer window, and you learned how to visit **Web sites** and use hyperlinks to move around. You also learned how to navigate by using the History list, and you learned how to search the Web for information.

Topic B In this topic, you learned how to use **tabbed browsing** to keep more than one page open in one browser window. You learned how to use **Quick Tabs** and how to save home tabs. You also learned how to disable tabbed browsing.

Topic C In this topic, you learned how to do basic **searches** and how to narrow your search. You learned about Google and about specific searches for images, news, and maps, and you learned how to do conversions and calculations.

Topic D In this topic, you customized Internet Explorer. You added sites to your **Favorites** list. You also deleted your **browser history** to protect your privacy. Then you added an **RSS feed** to Internet Explorer.

Topic E In this topic, you accessed **multimedia content** on the Web. You played audio and video in Windows Media Player embedded in the browser.

Review questions

1 Which component of the Internet Explorer window do you use to enter a URL?

2 Which feature allows you to enter a URL in the Address bar without having to type the entire address?

3 Why would you use the History list?

4 Name at least two popular Web search engines.

5 What feature allows you to store the addresses of Web sites you visit frequently?

6 How is audio and video content from the Web displayed on your computer?

7 True or false? The Add to Favorites button in Internet Explorer also provides a command to organize your Favorites list.

8 True or false? You can subscribe to RSS feeds on only those sites that offer that service.

9 Which of the following are in the Favorites Center in Internet Explorer 8? [Choose all that apply.]

A RSS Feeds

B Home Page settings

C Add-in programs

D Browsing history

E Windows Messenger

10 True or false? You can have only 10 tabs open at a time.

11 True or false? You can disable tabbed browsing if you don't want to use it.

12 What's the difference between entering two terms with quotation marks around them and entering the same terms without quotation marks?

13 True or false? Using proper capitalization helps when you're searching on someone's name.

14 How can you search for sites that both have certain terms and don't have other terms?

Independent practice activity

In this activity, you will practice using Internet Explorer 8 features like Favorites, RSS feeds, the History list, and tabbed browsing.

1 Open a news Web site such as `www.cnn.com` or `www.bbc.com`. Add this page to your favorites, creating a **News** folder to put it in. Open two other news sites and add them to your favorites in the News folder.

2 Using one of the news sites that you added to your Favorites list, subscribe to an RSS feed. Many sites have RSS feed links. See if you can subscribe to a specific news subject that interests you.

3 Open the History list in the Favorites Center. Use the History tab's drop-down list to examine the visited sites in different orders.

4 Open two or three sites with similar topics (e.g., movie review sites). Save the tab group in your favorites by clicking the Add Current Tabs to Favorites button and choosing Add Tab Group to Favorites.

5 Close all but one tab.

6 Set new tabs to open to your home page. (Use the tab settings accessible through Internet Options.)

7 Close Internet Explorer.

Course summary

This summary contains information to help you bring the course to a successful conclusion. Using this information, you will be able to:

A Use the summary text to reinforce what you've learned in class.

B Determine the next courses in this series (if any), as well as any other resources that might help you continue to learn about Windows 7.

Topic A: Course summary

Use the following summary text to reinforce what you've learned in class.

Unit summaries

Unit 1

In this topic, you learned how to **log on** to a Windows 7 computer, identified the **desktop components**, and learned how to use the mouse. Next, you used the **Start menu** to open applications and used the **taskbar** to switch between open applications. Then, you learned how to move and resize **windows**, use the Control menu buttons, and work with menus, toolbars, and dialog boxes. Then, you learned how to use **Windows Help and Support**. Finally, you locked your computer and logged off.

Unit 2

In this topic, you learned that data is stored in files, and each file is stored in a **folder**. Files and folders are organized in a folder hierarchy, with C: as the root folder. You learned that **libraries** are collections of related folders or other locations, and that folders can belong to several libraries. You learned how to navigate in the folder hierarchy, create folders, and rename folders. Next, you created, saved, printed, moved, copied, deleted, and restored files, and you opened files in their associated applications.

Unit 3

In this topic, you learned how to change the way Windows Explorer arranges and displays files and other objects. You also learned how to edit a file's **metadata**. Then, you learned how to search for content on your computers. You learned why Windows **indexes** some folders to speed searching. You learned about the difference between a Start menu search and a Windows Explorer search, and you learned how to search the file contents in non-indexed locations. Finally, you learned how to save searches.

Unit 4

In this topic, you customized your desktop and Start menu. You created **shortcuts** on the desktop and **pinned icons** to the Start menu and taskbar. You also unpinned icons and removed shortcuts. Next, you learned how to add, move, and remove Windows **gadgets**, and change a gadget's settings. Then, you customized some of your **system settings** by using the **Control Panel**. You set properties for your mouse and keyboard. Finally, you changed your desktop background, selected a new screen saver, and adjusted the sound.

Unit 5

In this topic, you browsed the World Wide Web by using **Internet Explorer**. You learned about the components of the Internet Explorer window, and you learned how to visit **Web sites** and use **hyperlinks** to navigate. You also learned how to use the **History** list. Next, you learned how to use **tabbed browsing**, use Quick Tabs, save home tab groups, and disable tabbed browsing. Next, you learned how to do a basic search and how to narrow your searches. Then, you added sites to your **Favorites** list, deleted your browsing history to protect your privacy, and added an **RSS feed**. Finally, you used Windows Media Player to play **multimedia content** on the Web.

Topic B: Continued learning after class

It is impossible to learn to use any software effectively in a single day. To get the most out of this class, you should begin working with Windows 7 to perform real tasks as soon as possible. We also offers resources for continued learning.

Next courses in this series

This is the first course in this series. The next course in this series is:

- *Windows 7: Advanced*

Other resources

For more information, visit www.axzopress.com.

Glossary

Active application
The application that is running in the foreground. Its window is not covered by any other application's window, and it is not minimized to a taskbar button.

Background application
An application that is not the foreground application. It could be minimized to a taskbar button or its window could be covered by another application's window.

Button
A clickable element. Buttons are identified by text, graphics, or both. They are typically bordered, though sometimes the border is not visible until you point to it with the mouse pointer.

Context menu
A menu that appears when you right-click an object. Also called a "shortcut menu."

Control Panel
The Windows program that you use to customize Windows and change system settings.

Cookie
A text file stored on your computer by a Web site you visit. Cookies are used to personalize your Web surfing experience.

Desktop
The Windows user interface element that lies behind all your applications, the Start menu, taskbar, and so forth.

E-mail
A system for transmitting text and rich-text messages across the Internet.

File extension
The portion of the file name that comes after the period; it's usually three letters long.

Gadget
A simple utility program with a small interface that sits on the Windows desktop.

Home folder
The top-level folder of the hierarchy that stores your personal documents and information.

Hyperlink
A clickable element on a Web page. Clicking a hyperlink takes you to other Web pages or to other locations on the current page.

Library
In Windows 7, a named collection of one or more folders grouped for organizational purposes. Libraries appear in Windows Explorer like folders, but are not actually part of the folder hierarchy.

Path
The list of folders, starting at the root, that lead to a specific file. Each folder in the path is separated from the others by a backslash.

Screen saver
A program that runs when your computer is idle, displaying graphics or animations to hide your information and provide entertainment.

Shortcut
A pointer or reference to a program, folder, or file.

Start menu
The primary Windows menu from which you open programs.

Taskbar
The bar that is (typically) displayed across the bottom of your Windows desktop. The taskbar comprises the Start button, pinned icons, and the notification area.

Taskbar button
A button, on the taskbar, representing an open application.

URL
A Uniform Resource Locator, which is the address of a Web page.

User account
A collection of settings and preferences representing a user of the computer. You access your user account by selecting your user name on the logon screen and entering your password.

Web browser
The program you use to access the World Wide Web. Internet Explorer is a Web browser.

Web page
A document created with the HTML coding language and made available on the Internet.

Window

A rectangular area of the screen containing the output from a program. Windows typically have a border, title bars, scrollbars, a status bar, and an area for the application's menus, buttons, and content.

Index

K

L

M

N

P

Q

R

S

T

U

V

W